BULLRUSH!

A Celebration of the Great New Zealand Game

For Justin –
Hope you enjoy
this peak @
Kiwi culture through
the lens of "Bullrush."
♡ Aroha

18/8/15

HarperCollins*Publishers*

First published in 2015
by HarperCollins*Publishers* (New Zealand) Limited
Unit D1, 63 Apollo Drive, Rosedale, Auckland 0632,
New Zealand
harpercollins.co.nz

HarperCollins*Publishers*

Unit D1, 63 Apollo Drive, Rosedale, Auckland 0632,
New Zealand
Level 13, 201 Elizabeth Street, Sydney NSW 2000,
Australia
A 53, Sector 57, Noida, UP, India
1 London Bridge Street, London, SE1 9GF,
United Kingdom
2 Bloor Street East, 20th floor, Toronto,
Ontario M4W 1A8, Canada
195 Broadway, New York NY 10007, USA

A catalogue record for this book is available from the
National Library of New Zealand.
ISBN 978 1 7755 4078 6 (paperback)
ISBN 978 1 7754 9115 6 (ebook)

Cover and internal design by Book Design,
www.bookdesign.co.nz
Cover image © Bettmann/Corbis
Typeset in PMN Caecilia
Printed and bound in Australia by Griffin Press

The papers used by HarperCollins in the manufacture
of this book are a natural, recyclable product made
from wood grown in sustainable plantation forests.
The fibre source and manufacturing processes meet
recognised international environmental standards,
and carry certification.

Photo / illustration credits
Bettmann/Corbis: pages 21, 72, 86
Devonport Primary School: pages 6, 7, 62, 70, 71, 89,
90, 96, 100, 112, 119, 129, 136, 139, 159, 165, 227, 234
Gordon McBride: pages 1, 61, 92, 202, 204, 207, 210
istock: pages iv, 2, 14, 22, 30, 40, 45, 47, 51, 52, 53, 55,
59, 67, 77, 78, 102, 109, 153, 166, 173, 183
Murray Webb/Alexander Turnbull Library: pages 107
(DCDL-0012333), 121 (DX-001-317)
Sam Mayhew: pages 212, 213, 221, 225
Shutterstock: pages 34, 49, 216
Swanson Primary School: pages 186, 191, 193
Tom Scott: page 63

BULLRUSH!

A Celebration of the Great New Zealand Game

DAVID SLACK

HarperCollins*Publishers*

Contents

1
The most FUN we EVER had

'Nothing in life is so exhilarating as to be shot at without result,' Winston Churchill said. That was bullrush. That was how it felt when you were winning.

Ahead of you was a wall of kids, ready to bring you down. Beyond them was your goal line, and safety. They would call your name. Their job was to put you on the ground. Your job was to get past them.

You'd come bursting over the line. You might be ducking, weaving, zipping, sidestepping. You might just be lumbering like a lorry. You might get torn down, maybe with a heap of kids on top of you.

But there were times when you might not. You would slip past them all, and as you made for the line, you'd be pumped. You'd be laughing, chucking a bit of cheek back over your shoulder as you showed them your heels.

You had been shot at without result. It felt just as good as Winston said it would.

Then, as you hit the line, someone would yell 'Bullrush!' and everyone waiting behind the line would follow you down in a shrieking, yelling, laughing cloud of arms and legs and shirts waiting to be ripped.

You might have buried yourself inside that cloud, pretending you weren't there, hoping no-one would see you. Or you might be making a noisy target of yourself.

It was exhilarating. Bullrush was the best game anyone had ever thought of, and we played it whenever we could. We played it at playtime, at lunchtime, after school, at the weekend. We played it whenever we could get a few people together.

You didn't need a ref, you didn't need a whistle, you didn't need a ball, you didn't need any special gear to play. All you needed was a decent stretch of grass.

Some of us didn't even need that. They played on asphalt at Lytton Street school in Feilding. Peter FitzSimons says he played it on the unforgiving wooden floor of a church hall, and didn't especially love it. A radio listener told me you haven't played bullrush until you've played it in the exercise yard at Paparua prison.

Here is the genius of bullrush: it doesn't matter whether you're good, middling, or completely useless at it. You can be a winner and a loser in the space of a few minutes, and so can everybody else. If you're accustomed to being called last when they're picking teams, this is the one time when you might get picked almost straight away. It amounts to more or less the same insult, sure, but it can be nice to go first for a change. Bullrush is for everyone.

You ask people what they remember of it and they start by saying 'Nothing', and then gradually they recall a little more, and a little more, and it all comes back to them and they love it.

My own memories are fragments. At Kiwitea Primary, a country school of eighty boys and girls, ten miles from Feilding, farms a hundred miles in every

It was a game that never
took itself too seriously.
It's a happy game,
it's a comedy on grass.

direction, we lined up for assembly every day on a concrete square. When it was over, we would march back to class with one of the big kids beating some kind of drum. There might have been a flag-raising. The war had been over for twenty years but its shadow was long, and there was another one going on in Vietnam to fight the evil Communists, and the Americans were making sure we were safe, and our own soldiers were helping them.

We had black-and-white movies from the National Film Unit. We listened to dreary broadcasts to schools on the National Programme at the hour now filled by Simon Mercep. There was the smell of the Gestetner machine, as it turned out its purple pages of newsletters and handouts; the smell of the fire in the potbelly stove; the smell of chlorine. The best smell of all was a row of gum trees alongside the swimming pool.

My nose registered more than my eyes. I needed milk-bottle-thick glasses when I was still a toddler, but no-one realised until I was seven. This is how I explain being tragically uncoordinated and entirely useless at ball sports.

Possibly, I also lacked common sense. Even without glasses I could see the pity in the other parents' eyes at seven-a-side rugby and on calf club day. Dad told me often there was no future in farming. I think, now, what he was saying gently was *There's no future in farming for you.*

I don't remember when I first played bullrush, and I can only recall flashes of it. I can remember it often involved getting my glasses broken, which might explain the flashes.

What I also remember is that bullrush, like so many things, was something you just picked up as you went along. There was no formal induction, no explanation. Suddenly, it would just be happening.

There is the education the teacher sets out for you in clear steps in the classroom, and then there is the education you acquire in the playground.

The playground can be a mystery. You watch the big kids, you listen, you try to make sense of it. Something happens spontaneously, a game begins, no-one really explains it, you just follow their lead, you go where it seems you have to go, you run when it seems you have to run, you yell when you think you're supposed to do that.

You have not the first idea what they're doing and what you're supposed to do.

The first time I saw a boy get the strap, I was standing at the end of a line of six with my hand out. You follow the bigger kids, you take their lead. After swimming, in the changing sheds, when the big boys asked if we knew how to milk the cow we said yes, but it turned out to be nothing like we'd seen done before on the farm.

I don't remember now whether we each had hold of our own penis or whether the big boys were holding them for us, but when he looked in to find out what was taking us so long the headmaster seemed to think we were doing it entirely the wrong way, and it seemed to matter quite a lot.

We stood in his office and he came down the line, each of the bigger boys getting six of the best. The office was quiet and each slap was startlingly loud. He stopped at the boy before me. We were free to go. I had only the vaguest idea what had happened. It became clear enough in time. My mother returned to teaching after fourteen years and discovered the children were using new and unfamiliar slang. She asked us one night, 'What's a wanker?'

You haven't played bullrush until you've played it in the exercise yard at Paparua prison.

So much of what passes from kid to kid is never written down, never entered in any book. The ball remains perpetually in the air. The swear words, the games, the rules — all of them pass from one to the next. There was no book of rules for bullrush, no *Bullrush Annual*, no trophy. But year after year, it got passed along, and you played your first game of bullrush just by following the others, taking your place at the line alongside them and waiting to see what happened.

Everyone loved it. Almost everyone. Robyn Malcolm liked it, sort of. But when she thinks about school and sports, she thinks mostly of the sorry excuse for a teacher who jogged around the 400-metre track behind her, taunting. Robyn was a small, round girl, running slowly. Bringing up the rear of a running race, she was mortified to have the teacher drop in behind. 'Come on, Robyn, faster, Robyn, how are you going, Robyn?' he mocked, flailing his arms, theatrically kicking up his feet, playing to the laughing children watching the spectacle. She enjoyed library and drama classes very much more.

Two geek friends, Nat and Jenine, say they couldn't see the point of it. Nat played it at Leigh School, often but always reluctantly. It was dull, it was thuggish, it seemed a bit stupid. He was always pleased when it was over and he could go back to doing something interesting. Jenine grew up in the USA. She says bullrush sounds a lot like Smear the Queer, which was a tiresome and unlovely thing.

But we all love to play in some way. At their annual Foo Camp technology gathering Nat and Jenine and a hundred or so ferociously smart people all play a kind of poker game, mixed with Cluedo and sci-fi, called Werewolf. It involves drinking, wits, and some playing cards. You can dazzle everyone with your skill, if you possess it, but no-one minds if you play appallingly badly. There's tension, there are players beating impossible odds, and there are gales of laughter. It's more or less bullrush, sitting down.

Play, the best kind of play, is life unleashed. We love the joy of it, the thrill of it, the risk. In bullrush, maybe what we loved most of all was the sheer fun of it. We were laughing the whole time. It was a game that never took itself too seriously. It's a happy game, it's a comedy on grass. We couldn't get enough of it.

And then one day they banned it, the fools. Or did they? We will answer this question by starting with Plato and moving forward at extreme speed.

2
Forever young

The great philosopher Plato may have played bullrush. Who can say for certain that he did not? History tells us that at the Isthmian Games, he wrestled. Maybe he also competed in the chariot races, or joined in the singing, or tried a little boxing. Maybe he tried pankration, which combined boxing and wrestling and had almost no rules except for: no biting, and no gouging eyes.

Children of Ancient Greece played hide and seek, blind man's buff, tag. Given any chance at all, children play. They always have, everywhere. In the face of poverty, in the midst of war, despite disease, despite disaster, even in slavery.

America's first people played bounce-on-the-rock; kicking-the-stick; singing games; chasing games; games that imitated animals. The colonists brought new ones with them. They danced around the maypole, they played leapfrog, they played some form of baseball. They also enjoyed cockfighting and cock throwing, an entertainment for the whole family, although that was a special treat, restricted to the holidays.

Contrary to their unpopular image, even the Puritans were up for fun: sex, beer, sports and games. Not everything enjoyable was a sin. If beer or sex or skittles helped keep your mind off a mortal sin like gluttony or idleness, then you really should go right ahead, in moderation, with your spouse, at the appropriate time, after the chores were done.

Why do we play? Consider the work of Brian Sutton-Smith, born in Wellington, 1924, graduate of Wellington Teachers College, graduate of Victoria University and UC Berkeley, with a doctorate in educational psychology from the University of New Zealand, one of the world's great authorities on children, games and play.

He catalogued the childhood histories of generations of New Zealanders, which we're about to explore. He spent a lifetime considering the serious business of play: What is it? Why does it mean so much to us? What purpose does it serve?

He said: 'We study play because life is crap. Life is crap, and it's full of pain and suffering, and the only thing that makes it worth living — the only thing that makes it possible to get up in the morning and go on living — is play.'

He also said: 'The opposite of play is not work. It's depression.'

The sound of children at play lifts your soul. There are people who live near schools and complain about the noise they make. No doubt they also complain that the sunset makes it hard for them to enjoy *Downton Abbey*.

If you give them the opportunity, children will play. If you give adults the opportunity, they tell children when, where and how they can do it. This may not necessarily be a good idea.

Play sits mostly at the edge of recorded history, because for most of human history, adults saw it as trivial. They left it to the children to do as they liked. And then things changed. Social reformers, in the past century or so, used play for what we might call social engineering. Play, they believed, might be educational, it might be therapeutic, it might make good citizens.

Or it might be a civil hazard. In New York City, at the end of the 19th century, Europe's huddled masses filled the streets, and orphaned and abandoned children survived however they could in slums and alleys. They worked long hours in sweat-houses, and played in those same slums and alleys. People took fright. Officials made it a crime to play in the streets.

Hundreds of children were arrested. Very quickly, avoiding arrest became a game in itself. The playing never stopped.

Privileged classes of the 19th century saw games as character forming. They might instil moral and patriotic qualities in a young man. You can slip this thought quite easily into a soldier's uniform. 'The Battle of Waterloo,' Englishmen would say proudly, 'was won on the playing fields of Eton.'

You might also blame Eton for sending 600 men *into the jaws of Death, into the mouth of Hell*. The Eton Game is an elaborate business played to this day in no place on earth but Eton. It looks a little like rugby, a little like cricket, slightly like Aussie Rules and, some people say, quite a lot like the Charge of the Light Brigade.

'We study play
because life is crap.'

Brian Sutton-Smith

Once you come to see play as something other than trivial, you then consider what particular benefits it might offer. Perhaps play will make them burn up excess energy. Perhaps it will help them learn.

Fifty years ago, Brian Sutton-Smith was writing that playground games were being used to make good citizens. Society didn't require its members to be outstanding at a game, they wanted them to learn, through playing games, to be competent social mixers, with a spirit of gamesmanship.

Reformers integrated playgrounds into housing estates, they made adventure playgrounds for disadvantaged children living in the concrete jungle. They embraced studies that showed a playing student makes a better student.

But by the end of his long academic career, Brian Sutton-Smith was posing a new question: Are the adults spoiling it? Are they intruding too much?

Play can be all kinds of things, he said. It can be an exercise in power. It can be an act of imagination. It can be a claim for identity. It can be just what you do for kicks. It can be very, very hard to define.

It can be a mistake to get too prescriptive about how, where and what children should do in their play. What's more appealing: a blank canvas and paints, or a drawing of a Disney character to colour in?

Games are rites of passage, he also said. 'The player performs a task, gains acceptance of his comrades and experiences success. It's playing out an analogy of life.'

You lived in a tribe or a village, you had your festivals and games and in those festivals and those games, you would do what someone told you, along with everyone else.

It's time to visit a fighting pit.

3
Wild colonials

The 19th-century New Zealand school had no whiteboard, no Google, no gluten-free lunchboxes, but it did have a fighting pit.

Yes, a fighting pit. It might be in the school, it might be in the paddock next door. You rolled up your sleeves and you took your argument to the pit. What happened outside the classroom stayed out there. The teacher didn't care.

If the big boys fancied a fight, there'd be a fight. Losing wouldn't be the end of your misery, either, because then you would be crowned. You would be patted three times on the back by the victor, who would then spit over your head — usually aiming too low.

Children, forever, have been angels, and forever they have been very, very wicked.

The 19th-century children of New Zealand didn't just pick fights with other kids, they made life unhappy for adults. To taunt a Chinaman, evil devil from the Orient that he was, you might throw your cap on the ground, clasp your hands in front, bow your head and trot around on tiptoe in a shuffling manner to ape his gait. Naughty children would play pranks, they would throw stones, they would raid orchards, they would steal chickens, they would go to the wharf to see the cattle landed and collect new swear words.

The streets were full of these monsters, and something had to be done. The nation's schools were opened, free of charge to every child in the 1870s, not out of a sense of noble purpose so much as to get semi-feral ratbags off the street. Their parents couldn't afford to pay for an education, so the state would do it and get them all rounded up and out of the way. By the end of the decade, school was compulsory.

For the next decade or two, the school playground was owned and ruled by the children. They played for keeps. There was any amount of rough play and there was the fighting pit. The likelihood that the big guy and the bully might pick on the little kid was very strong.

Despite the violence, despite the tyranny of thugs, this was an opportunity to make their own fun, with enough kids to make it entertaining. Brian Sutton-Smith described it as the golden age of play for New Zealand kids.

Pioneer kids hadn't had that opportunity. The first decades of European settlement were meagre. Your exciting new life in New Zealand might begin with a bullock, a wagon and the hope that in due course you could afford some chickens and a cow. Children would be hard at work. If they found any spare time, they might use it to explore their surroundings, do things with their knife, make a shanghai, swim, climb trees, go eeling.

They had nowhere to congregate. Compulsory schooling changed all that. The schoolyard became the centre of their play world. They had hundreds, thousands of games, and they would blend and change constantly.

They played by their rules, they played whatever they chose to play, and if you were the biggest and strongest you decided how things would be. Play was sometimes brutal, and the most dangerous game of all was Shinty. It was hockey played with extreme prejudice. Like hockey, you used the stick to swipe a ball towards the goal. Unlike hockey, there were no rules about how you did that. You had a stick of any kind at all; it might be made of iron. You could swing it any way you liked, any time you liked, at anything you didn't like. It was a wonder, people said, that a head was never caved in.

The kids loved it. It would be a craze for a while, someone would get badly hurt and it would be banned for a time but it would never be gone for long. *Shinty one, hockey two, shinty three and away* they would chant, and off you went, into a world of pain. This was not a game for sooks. All the skin was off their shins. There were often black eyes. You might lose a finger.

Bullrush was also more violent in the 19th century and, aside from Shinty, the most popular of games. There were also many like it. In Colours, if the colour you've chosen is called by the player in the middle, you try to get past him to the far side. Please Jack May We Cross Your Golden River was the same; so was Nigger Boys, in which the player in the middle nominates the number of nigger boys he wants to come across. Lessons on civil rights, racism or bigotry are rarely mentioned in recollections of the time.

This was not a game for sooks. All the skin was off their shins. There were often black eyes. You might lose a finger.

Many of the games had British origins, certainly bullrush did — they knew it back Home as British Bulldog. You packed your trunk, you packed your memories, you sailed for a new land. When you had a picnic — and in pioneer life that was one of the things you looked forward to most — you played the games of Home. The ball stays in the air and makes its way into the colonial playground.

When you weren't playing variations on bullrush, you might be conducting initiation games. You might be blindfolded and ordered to 'peewee some more yet' into another boy's cap. The cap would, of course, turn out to be your own.

Or you might be writing romantic verse. One group of Dunedin boys — some glorious morning in 1900, according to a reminiscence shared with Brian Sutton-Smith — sent out to write poems, returned with nothing, while the girls recited poems about the wind in the playground, the flowers and the sun. The boys, duly punished for their laziness, had in fact been busy. Each had begun his own poem but one of the boys captured their imagination with the opening line: *I've got a dog called Jack and he's got a cast-iron cock*. They had thrown themselves into creating an epic, but you could hardly let the teacher see it.

In this era there were no major sports. But towards the end of the century, more educators were seeing sport as valuable to child development. The teachers came out onto the playing field, with a whistle around their neck and a rule book in their pocket. Shinty gave way to hockey and rugby, rounders to cricket.

It had begun with military drill. The 1877 Education Act required teachers to make provision for physical drill. In practice, that tended to be taught by military instructors, soldiers no longer fighting land wars, men with not much of a teaching background. They sometimes combined drill classes with the duties of school caretaker.

Mr Patrick Walsh of Invercargill, formerly a sergeant of the Royal Irish Fusiliers, was — as reported in *A History of Children's Play: The New Zealand Playground 1840–1950* — 'generally armed with a short length of broom handle and on one occasion pursued a school inspector who dared to criticise his methods. He pursued the latter with stick and lurid language.'

The role of play in the curriculum steadily expanded and would have the perverse effect of narrowing the range of activities children were involved in.

Military drill evolved into organised sports. Teachers came out to supervise the playgrounds, to coach children in organised sports, and the rougher games and practices disappeared.

First you play rugby at your school, then you challenge another school and before you know it, there are cups and competitions and trophies and school pride at stake. Teachers' chests burst with pride at great wins and the playgrounds came to be dominated by rugby and cricket. At its peak in the 1920s and 1930s this sports trophy mania would militate against playing almost anything else.

The other great change would be a commercial one. A lot can change when people discover something has a buck in it. From 1920 onward, the toy business exploded. Mass production and advertising put an affordable toy in almost every child's hands. If someone else is making your toys, you're doing less of your own play, you're doing less inventing of your own games.

At the middle of the 20th century, Brian Sutton-Smith described a playground free from physical aggression, a calmer place in which to play.

The modern school child was 'typically a dilettante of games'. He played plenty of them, in PE, in the hall, in the playground. Unless he was destined to be a sportsman, he didn't do long hours of training. He just had to be capable of having fun with other kids. A game was a test of your social skills rather than your physical prowess.

The kids were doing a whole lot of playing, but if you looked closely, you could see it was the adults making most of the play.

Why take a glass of
water when you can
bury your fangs in
a jugular?

4
Who's AFRAID
of bullrush?

'I went out to a celebration at a Sikh temple in Takanini,' says Len Brown, in his 28th-floor meeting room looking out over Auckland city. 'They said, "Oh, come out the back at the end of the service and you can watch kabaddi," and — it had got completely lost in translation — I thought we were going to go out the back and have a cup of tea.

'Well, anyhow, they took me out the back to a back field and on the field there's this great big round circle about half the size of an AFL field and in the middle of it they had these people stripped down to shorts, top uncovered, and they were playing this game *kabaddi*.'

You have a team that is trying to defend against another team. They have to hold each other and then one person comes off the back and you've got to tackle that person who's trying to go over the line. Or something like that. If you saw it, he says, you'd say it was bullrush. Or at least a tag game that looks an awful lot like it.

'You actually have to pin them. It's not just a tackle and that's it, no, you actually have to pin them and stop them from getting over, so it's a bullrush wrestling game, and it's *full on*.' The guys who succeed best are very heavily built, like wrestlers, he says, and they have liquid acceleration.

There is raiding, like bullrush, there is the challenge of catching a raider. If you catch a raider and he loses his chanting breath '… *kabaddi, kabaddi, ka…*', he's out. What you need,

it seems above all, is stamina and lung power. You have to be able to hold your breath for a very long time.

Kabaddi is very, very old. It originated in ancient India. It's the national game of Bangladesh and Nepal. There are world championships. New Zealand has sent a team but so far no country but India has won.

Let's try the German version of bullrush, *Wer hat Angst vorm schwarzen Mann?*, which they have been playing for at least a few hundred years. Or, in English, Who's Afraid of the Black Man? Yes, really. Scholars suggest this is a reference to the Black Death. Or perhaps it just faithfully preserves the way a lot of people used to talk.

Here's how you play Who's Afraid of the Black Man?, as described by a German school kid. You need one black man and up to thirty children (or more), and a playing field with two lines. Choose a hunter — the Black Man. He stands on one of the lines and the other pupils stand on the other line, which is on the other side of the playground.

The Black Man asks: 'Who's afraid of the Black Man?' The players answer:

'Nobody!' Black Man: 'And what if he comes?' Players: 'Then we'll run away!' This is your cue to run to the other side of the playground. The Black Man runs to the other side, too, and while he runs, he tries to catch you. Whoever is caught becomes his assistant and helps him to catch the others.

YouTube footage suggests, and German acquaintances confirm, that this is and always has been a tagging game, no tackling.

This is a recurring theme as you cross the world looking for a similar game to bullrush. Tackling happens here, it happens in Australia, it happens in the UK, but it doesn't appear to happen anywhere else.

In Canada and the United States they have been playing Red Rover since it crossed the seas from Britain. They played it in Australia and often called it Cocky Laura.

You form two teams, or as one bitter person recalled it: 'Divide the children into teams based on the most socially acceptable way of destroying self-esteem.' You link hands with your team-mates. Each team lines up facing the other, holding hands, standing apart. You need some room to build up a running start.

Divide the children into teams based on the most socially acceptable way of destroying self-esteem.

One team will shout, 'Red Rover, Red Rover, send [name] right over!' That person lets go of their team-mates' hands and hurtles towards the other team, hoping to break through their hands. If they succeed, they get to go back to their own team and take an opposing player with them. If they fail, they have to join the other side.

Then the other team will shout, 'Red Rover, Red Rover, send ...' and it goes back and forth until one team has only one person left. The prospects of a damaged wrist are decently greater than zero.

Russia and other nations of the former USSR play Ali Baba. Hungary knows it as *Adj, király, katonát!* and in the Czech Republic it's *Král vysílá své vojsko*, all of them more or less Red Rover with a different name.

The tamest version in all the world is probably the Japanese version, *Hana Ichi Monme*. Children split into two teams; they all hold hands, face each other in two lines. Then they step forward and back according to the rhythm of a song. Each time the song ends, the team leaders step forward and do *janken*, which is essentially rock-paper-scissors.

The winner goes back to their team, and they discuss who the team wants to add from the other team. After they have decided, they sing another song doing the same movement and announce the person they want.

One team sings *We're so happy we won, hana ichi monme.*

The other sings *We're so upset we lost, hana ichi monme.*

The winning team, nominating one player, sings *We want that kid.*

The other sings *We don't understand which kid you mean.*

It carries on in this delicate way for a very long time. Risk of a child coming to any harm: so close to zero, it's immeasurable.

All fun, but honestly, this is tame stuff. The way we did it was way more interesting. Why take a glass of water when you can bury your fangs in a jugular?

5
TRAMPLED
underfoot

In the 1980s we couldn't get enough of waterbeds and indoor cricket. You can still get a waterbed today, you can still play indoor cricket, but both are strictly for the enthusiasts.

It was a hoot, that indoor cricket. The rules and the scoring were nice and simple and all you really needed to know was the difference between a bat and a ball. You could have a bit of a belt around, even if you were completely hopeless. You would get up a team with your mates, maybe your workmates, and you'd have a great time; a few laughs, a bit of joshing, a few drinks afterwards.

It was vastly better for office morale than any of those bullshit courses where you'd have to shut your eyes and fall backwards into the waiting arms of Julie the product manager, Wayne the accountant and Mary-Anne who couldn't stand the sight of you.

It looked, for a while, as though it might be the same fun as bullrush: a game where everyone's laughing. Bullrush let you be a star but if you weren't, nobody minded. You could be quite useless, and it would have no bearing on the outcome. To begin with, it seemed that in indoor cricket, just like bullrush, nobody minded if you were really, really bad at it. Everyone was having a laugh.

But it didn't last. There was a score to be achieved. That score mattered. It had to be better than the other side, because *we're here to win, aren't we?* It didn't take too long before the keen players were getting quietly irritated with you, because *they're creaming us and not looking at anyone but, mate, how could you drop that?* You weren't leading, you weren't following, and you couldn't get out of the way. You mattered to their fate, and even though this was supposed to be a knock-around bit of fun, winning mattered, dammit. It's not easy finding the game for everyone.

But bullrush, well, bullrush welcomed you. There was a role for you, even if it was just to crumple to your knees at the first hint of trouble.

It didn't begin so sweetly. In those early New Zealand schoolyards it was a tag game with kicking, punching and sometimes a full-on pummelling.

It went by many names: King Seenie, Horney, Blackthorn, King O'Weenie, King's Den, perhaps most commonly Bar the Door.

Brian Sutton-Smith reports even more names for it: Bar the Gate, Black Bull Bee, Broken Barley, By the Door, Free Pass, Goosey, Goosey Up and Down, Holding, King Caesar, King Caesar's Den, King Dick, King O'Seenie, Last Man Over, Last Call, Punch King, Punch King Seenio, Red Rover, Running through the Middle.

Whatever you called it, there would be one lonely boy in the middle whose job was to catch or tag players as they came hurtling towards him and stop them from getting to the other end of the playing field. Once you'd been caught, you joined the taggers in the middle, until everyone else had been tagged.

Or not. In another version, you could free all the players in the middle by kicking an object like a tin or a can through to the other side.

'I can't quite decipher between my memories of playing the actual game and my nightmares of playing it.' Jacinda Ardern

In some versions, the 'tag' you got from the player in the middle might actually be three punches on the back. Naturally, whenever the tagging was done that way, the question of how hard you punched became important. Do it too hard, and you've got a fight.

One game, Punch King, was vaguely like bullrush but a whole lot more violent. You and your team lined up with your backs to the wall. The other team had to pull you forward, over a line, just a couple of paces ahead. Simple enough, but here's the tricky bit: you were only allowed to get them forward by pulling them but they were allowed to stop you by punching you. Any kind of punch was allowed. Plenty were below the belt.

Some versions involved crowning. As you were making your run past the tagger — King Seenie — his aim would be to crown you while saying the words *One, two, three, you're the man for me.* King Seenie would be careful how he did it, because there was a good chance you might bite his hands, or belt him, to stop him from getting his filthy paws on your head.

Or the kids in the middle might have you pinned down, three or four or five of them, as they took their time to pat your head and deliver a long chant.

If you managed to wriggle free for a moment, the whole ceremony would have to start again: *Keep him quiet, hold him down, pat him thrice upon the crown. Blackball, Blackball, Blackball, one, two, three, Joseph Jackson you are he.*

What happened to those crowning ceremonies? One suggestion is that they faded out with school caps. Another is that tackling displaced them.

With no teacher ever around, your chances of getting a hiding were good. If they didn't like you, they might let you be the last man standing and let you come across last. Then the crowd would fall on you, and every last kid would pile on. If you had been putting up a bit too strong a fight on your earlier trips, you might find you were down there for a while.

Naturally, once playgrounds were supervised, things got tamer. As schools steadily embraced organised sports and introduced cricket and rugby and basketball into the school programme, many games disappeared. But bullrush rolled on, sitting alongside rugby as the informal game the kids played at playtime, at lunchtime, on the same soft ground where they would play rugby.

Tackling in rugby was an obvious technique to use in bullrush. Where once you had to be tagged, now you had to be tackled. The two games fed each other. Bullrush was where you might first learn to sidestep, to weave, to fend.

It might seem hard to imagine now, but back in 1905 the sense of excitement and pride New Zealanders felt, discovering that their rugby team had travelled Home and beaten virtually all comers, was enormous. They had taken a game back to its place of birth and played it like masters. The young nation embraced the game, made it their own. Schools put greater and greater stock in the accomplishments of their rugby teams. The young rugby players, when they weren't playing the game itself, when they didn't have a ball and two teams of fifteen, and a referee, might well play a game of its nearest relation, bullrush.

What about the girls? Girls played bullrush too, didn't they? Yes, but much less so in the early years of New Zealand schools. In a tiny school with a roll of perhaps just a dozen, boys and girls would play together to make the numbers. But in larger ones, it was quite different. In many schools you would find a high concrete wall between the two playgrounds. Playing together was never encouraged and behind the walls the girls played quieter games — Oranges and Lemons, Farmer in the Dell, Ring a Ring o' Roses, Bingo. They played games for all ages, they played games that involved singing, games that used rhymes, games with a skipping rope, games concerned with marriage, with funerals, with couples.

But they also played chasing games, all kinds of tag games where a cat chases a mouse, a fox chases a goose, other versions of Bar the Door that used colours, names and guessing. But no punching, no scragging, no torn clothes.

Gradually, and mostly to do with the embrace of physical activity as being good for the children, girls became involved in more active games. As they did, they joined in boys' play, and in due course, in some places if not all, played bullrush together.

This was the moment at which my generation stepped out into the playground, and discovered a magnificent game.

was it?

PART TWO

6
A brief history of lunchtime

My grandmother had five sisters and two brothers. Her younger sister, Nan, lived longest. She would reminisce with my mother. There was a honeysuckle hedge near the house when she was a child. It was left to grow wild and the soft leaves, piled thickly, made a cushion: a long soft ride down to the ground as good as a playground slide. She said once to Mum: 'I wonder if my mother and father knew how happy I was.'

Mum remembers bullrush vividly. They called it Bar the Door. She was quite the athlete. She liked that she could outrun and outsmart the boys. What she

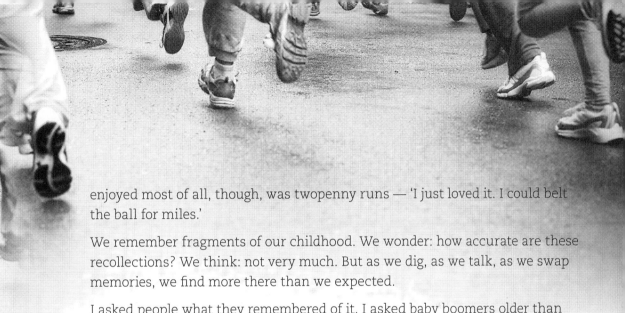

enjoyed most of all, though, was twopenny runs — 'I just loved it. I could belt the ball for miles.'

We remember fragments of our childhood. We wonder: how accurate are these recollections? We think: not very much. But as we dig, as we talk, as we swap memories, we find more there than we expected.

I asked people what they remembered of it. I asked baby boomers older than me, Gen X kids, millennials. What they all said first was: 'I don't remember much about bullrush.' But they would remember one thing, and that would bring another memory into focus and then another. They were happy memories. Reminiscing can take you on a warm holiday. This is where we went.

'I resembled a dolphin or possibly a fur seal, it's hard to say. Maybe a Bryde's whale.' Scotty Stevenson

7
Scotty Stevenson

Ruakaka Primary School,
Bream Bay College

1982–95

'It's the perfect sport, isn't it? There's a lovely balance between winning, losing, starting again, the challenge all in front of you again, and just when you think you've got an advantage, it turns on you. And there you go. No equipment required, just your wits and a bit of bravery.'

Scotty Stevenson loves sport, loves writing about it, loves watching it, doesn't believe in being too earnest about it. 'It should be fun. Even at the top level it's got to be fun. I know you've got to take the business seriously, but you don't have to be serious while you're taking it seriously.'

Still, it's a big deal. 'It's the greatest distraction in the world, sport. Let's be honest. It's the only extracurricular activity that has its own slot on the news.'

He loved to play bullrush, right up until the day it was banned. He first played it at Ruakaka Primary School on State Highway 1. The main field was right by the state highway, 'a chain-link fence up between us and the cars that drove past'. In winter it was muddy and they just kept playing because 'none of us wore shoes to school anyway so it didn't really matter'. It was good fun, it was something to do between arguing about playing marbles and trying to pash girls.

And then he was at Bream Bay College, and bullrush got a lot more interesting. 'We were a form one to seven school as well, so you took your chances. And you had to pick your battles because you could get crushed. Because that was the way of all things.'

Did it get violent? 'Of course. Yeah. Grudge match. This was a chance to get even. You could tell who was lining you up, so that added a certain frisson to the whole experience. You would try and put at least four bodies between you and the person who was after you. Which, you know, let's be honest, is what most people do these days anyway in all walks of life — just put four people between you and danger.'

There was strategising, plenty of it. 'Unfortunately, I was the overweight kid; I wasn't that fast, so the strategising going on usually involved putting me in front of someone else. I may have been the strategy as opposed to forming the strategy.'

He didn't really mind. Avoidance wasn't his policy in bullrush. He wasn't looking to bust the tackle, he wasn't looking to sidestep anyone.

He just tried to keep his head down and go as fast as he could. 'Which wasn't overly fast. I was much better in water. In that way I resembled a dolphin or possibly a fur seal, it's hard to say. Maybe a Bryde's whale.'

Always the toughest thing in bullrush was the start. Being the first guy in the middle always sucked. Unless you were a hero. 'The best guys always volunteered for the task as well, which I think summed them up; you know, the confident guys would always go "I'll have a crack first".

'But it was always embarrassing if you were to find yourself first in the middle if you didn't get a single person — having to line back up again and go *oh, I missed the entire school, this is just embarrassing.* I'm not entirely sure when that happened to me but I distinctly remember it happening.'

Does he remember people getting hurt? 'Yeah, but I was also at school at the height of World Wrestling Federation, so there was more danger of having a broken neck from being DDT'd on a tennis court than there was of being seriously injured in bullrush.'

There were tears every lunchtime, ripped uniforms, all the rest of it, sure, and the fear of playing bullrush, the adrenalin of playing, 'but I don't remember anyone being carted off to hospital. You got your scrapes and bruises and that was part of life.'

Why do we reminisce so fondly about bullrush? 'Because it was the ultimate proving ground in so many ways for people and for testosterone-laden kids. Of course, not for everyone, but there was always a champion. You always knew who the best was and the great thing in this age of participation as opposed to victory was that with bullrush, there could only ever be one result, mate, you either lost or you won. There was no second place.'

It might well be the ultimate sport for dummies. 'Imagine this as a global phenomenon. Someone asks, "How do you play it?" You say, "Oh, it's pretty easy, mate, someone just stands in the middle and tackles someone, then they stand in the middle and tackle everyone. There you go."'

'Well, what happens to the last guy?'

'Well, everyone tackles him.'

'Oh, perfect.'

This is is

Bullrush!

8
Tom Scott

Lytton Street Primary School, Feilding
1952–59

They played their bullrush on hard concrete. 'And even the school cripple, Mervyn Jaggard, with one withered leg from polio, he joined in. You go to a playground now and it's chips of rubber, and people are growing up soft. Charlie Upham today, having gone to a New Zealand primary school, would be lucky to win a Polar Medal. They're all soft.'

Young Tommy Scott played rugby but he was fatally short-sighted. 'I would play rugby with my glasses on so at least I could recognise my own team.' Contact sport is hard on your glasses. 'They were constantly held together with Elastoplast. Great wads of Elastoplast. And so bullrush was a bridge too far for me.'

He watched at the sidelines, just a bit of cheering at the snapping of fibulas and tibias and femurs and dislocating shoulder joints. 'It was an orthopaedic surgeon's dream, bullrush at Lytton Street Primary School.'

They lived on almost nothing, four miles out of town, in a farm labourer's cottage. Weekends, they roamed far and wide over the countryside. The very wealthy farmers on either side of them would throw away all sorts of amazing stuff: lounge suites, record players, old bicycles, tubas, bagpipes, piled high at the rubbish dump. 'We would drag it all home. You'd get amazing shit from their places. I got a World War One gas mask from one raid and brought that home. I was really impressed with that.' They'd fill the house up with it and the old man would go berserk.

He claims they also found the axle from the Crewe murder, the Lindbergh baby skeleton and remnants from the lost Amelia Earhart plane. 'The markings were pretty faded, but I'm pretty certain it was hers.'

All along the bank of the Oroua River there were huts made of flax and raupo, where tramps would sleep. There were still tramps then, in the fifties — unemployed men who would knock on the door and ask for a meal; swaggies like Russian Jack. 'And sometimes with a lonely housewife they would get sex as well as scones — but mostly a cup of tea and a scone.'

Just because you hadn't heard about it doesn't mean it didn't happen. 'You never came home to find your mother readjusting her clothing and saying, "Oh, Russian Jack's been here, what a lovely man"?'

They ran wild, the Scott kids. It made them special. 'All the other kids up the road, they all had Meccano sets, and they had Just William books, and they had Rupert the Bear annuals, Hornby train sets and stuff. But none of them wanted to play at their place. They wanted to come down to our house, which was just a tip. And we would make extraordinary things in the backyard of the things we collected.'

What kids want is a blank slate. 'They do! Our farmhouse was so bad that wallpaper had peeled off and there was just basically scrim in the bedrooms so Mum let us make paste out of flour and water and we'd put newspapers over the top of it. We ended up with papier-mâché walls and we were allowed to paint them how we liked, so I painted our bedroom. There were four of us in there. I painted an aquarium. I painted it blue. I painted seaweed and pirate's treasure, so our room was an undersea grotto.' He doesn't know what those other kids had on their walls. 'Framed pictures of the royal family and dried flower arrangements and shit? But they wanted to come down and swim in the aquarium. So our imaginations were allowed to run wild. There was no money so we had no toys. We made everything up. And we were better for it, I think.'

He would make jokes. Never rude enough to invite a thrashing, but enough to make the kids laugh and the teacher feel that they were on the receiving end. 'One time the teacher, Mr Sullivan, was showing us how to march. And he was a fat man — he drove the school bus — and he always smelled like he never washed his hands properly after going to the toilet — and he was showing us how to march. And he was marching up and down the classroom one day, a fat man going: "Left right right left wheel left wheel right left right". And I said: "Pull your stomach *innnn*, pull your stomach *innnn*. Who's a fat boy? Who's a fat boy?" I don't know why.

'And he just ran straight, ploughed through a sea of desks to get to me, whacking me around the head. He was incensed. *Stomach in! Pull stomach in!* And gee, I got a bit of a thrashing from him. Then he was deeply ashamed after it. He was sort of terrified I would go home and snitch on him. But I didn't.'

'There was no way through and yet if you are that kid, what a moment of pride.'

Te Radar

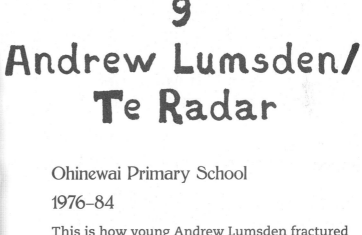

9
Andrew Lumsden/
Te Radar

Ohinewai Primary School
1976–84

This is how young Andrew Lumsden fractured his arm playing bullrush: 'What happened was they were running at me and I thought, I'll hop down this imaginary rabbit hole and hide.' But there was no rabbit hole.

'I don't know why I thought it was a rabbit hole. I love to think that at a young age my imagination was taking me away from the rigours of the rugger turf and the bullrush thing into this wonderful creative world, because there was a lot of standing around thinking about the punishment that was about to ensue. Because I wasn't the biggest kid, and chances were I was gonna get pummelled. And the worst thing was if you did get caught and depending on who caught you, then you faced the ordeal of the typewriter — if you remember that — which was a terrible thing — you know, you're knelt on by someone who pretended to type on your chest and if you laughed or anything then it was time to hit the return button, which was to whack you in the face.'

Was there a lot of that? 'I think sometimes people just dropped out of the game as and when they decided to catch someone they wanted to torment.'

Ohinewai was a small country school — maybe thirty or forty boys and girls playing. 'For some reason I always remember it being a summer thing. And in actual fact, I think it would have been better to have played it throughout the winter. Maybe I just remember summer because the field was harder and so the thought of landing on it underneath a pile of bodies was never pleasant.'

You might call it a sort of hunger games, but the good kind, where you can start afresh and go on. No dead kids, although you might have a few broken ones.

The imaginary rabbit hole didn't save him, and he was in a cast for a few weeks. He doesn't recall any other injuries but he's sure there were plenty. Leg taps, ankle trips, they were the nasty ones. It was very easy to have things go wrong. 'But being broken is a part of life as well — if you aren't careful or something goes wrong, bad things can happen to you.'

There were no umpires, no teachers. 'You created your own safety.' There wasn't a lot of refined tackling — it was much more brutal. There was scragging. There wasn't as much finesse to it as there was in controlled sports with referees; it was *bring them down however*. And it happened organically.

'It would start up with a few people and by the end of the day you'd have a vast number of people there and then it would sort of peter out and the lunch bell would ring and everyone would go back inside exhausted and covered in grass stains.'

He loves its life lessons — the underdog, the little kid, seeing the little kid pass the big kids and the ability for someone to bulldoze their way through with brute force and the fact that enormous mass can be brought down with the concerted efforts of a whole lot of little people. Or, alternatively, that if you really are pushing through that you just can go on and on, despite the clamouring and clutching straws of the people who would wish you to stop.

'So either way you can take that same action and read something different into it, which is also a great life lesson — everyone's looking at the same thing but people are getting a different picture. Some are willing it on, others are hoping for them to be stopped.'

When it became too big, people would drop out because it got a bit wild. 'But those wonderful moments when it got down to that last kid and there was no way through and yet if you are that kid, what a moment of pride, and that challenge of thinking *I can do it, I'm gonna do it, I'm gonna get through*.'

Every day there was every opportunity for someone to be the hero, the legend. Maybe no-one really targeted you, maybe the guys in the middle had been stalking other kids and you'd been quietly slipping through down the side of the field.

Or there might be humiliation. The way they played the game, the last kid would get caught and it would all start all over again, and that last kid would have to go into the middle. 'That was horrible, being the person who hadn't got caught, if you couldn't catch anyone.'

There was nothing quite like it, for getting around people and running through. Contact sport was the only thing that offered anything like it. 'Sometimes you think, *Oh I'd like to play that again.* But of course you never do.'

The closest he's come was a form of ball tag he played in Tokelau with school kids. He loved it. 'The white guy turns up. So he's going to be the target.' It all came back to him, the sense of people getting together and trying to knock people out. 'And then you become part of that team and then *you* can knock someone out.' What he'd also forgotten was how quickly you can change your allegiance to the rebellion. 'You're thinking — *I'm going to get through and I'm going to defy the wall of people stopping me* — to suddenly going *All right, no-one else is getting through.*'

It teaches you to be a mercenary. Or a lawyer. 'And it does show you that when you think that someone's with you and then suddenly for whatever reason they're not, they can become your worst enemy very quickly.' Perhaps, Ruth suggests, bullrush is *Animal Farm.* That would be Radar's wife, the witty, clever and not-at-all-sports-inclined Ruth Spencer, who was a library person at school. Library people were the only ones allowed to eat their lunch inside. She says it was the absolute best.

10
Michelle Langstone

Eastern Suburbs, Auckland

1985–95

They played it at primary school just one single
time. 'There was this boy who was the shortest
kid in our school, he was "it" in the middle.
The game started and someone ran into him
or he ran into somebody. His nose, it was
like someone turned on an outdoor hose tap.
Spraying crimson, all across the black asphalt.
And that was it. It was over before it started.'

There had been such huge anticipation. They were going to be allowed to play bullrush! Her dad gave her the best bullrush advice: When they blow the whistle, run like buggery. 'I remember kids being scared of it. Bullrush was talked about in whispers. It was like "The big kids are playing bullrush" — it was something you graduated into, a really big deal.'

But it never happened again. 'We did play bullrush in the school swimming pool at lunchtime. Everyone got in the water and it was the most impossibly slow game. I remember everybody wading desperately or diving underwater and banging into people. I wonder if it was an intermediary measure to make it available. But it was just the most boring thing in the world and everybody lost interest.

'At our high school I'm pretty sure it was banned. We had a one-metre rule between guys and girls at our high school. Oh my God, it was so uptight. It was a very sanitised school. They were very good at sport, very well presented and very good academic staff, but it was all very pristine, all very within code. Bullrush was just gone.'

But there was this amazing skate centre near Pakuranga called Skateaway. In the booths upstairs you could get rainbow shaved-ice drinks and watch the skaters. The elevated DJ booth right beside the skating rink was covered in furry material. The furry material was there so that when you played bullrush and got slammed into it, you wouldn't get hurt.

That's right, bullrush. You'd skate from one end to the other trying to get away and you'd go whack into the soft walls. 'They'd turn up the lights so everybody could see and everyone would just go hell for leather for twenty minutes. Then business would resume and the DJ would play the eighties music and everyone would just move on.'

Skateaway closed down before she was old enough to try bullrush, 'but then this other really miserable skating rink opened up somewhere near where we lived. That was the first day I ever played bullrush on skates. And that was the day I broke my wrist.'

They turned on the lights and *Okay, off you go.* Michelle skated carefully, cautiously, hesitantly right along the outside. Safe, but not safe enough. The guy who was 'it' and one of his mates just bowled into her, two of them at once; she landed on her wrist. *Great,* she thought.

'It was my moment and I was so disappointed. But the thing that actually struck me was: nobody stopped the game. I just got up and someone shunted me off and the manager of the place was like, "Oh right, broken your wrist, all right," as if it had happened seven hundred times, and the game kept going.

I looked down at my wrist 'cause I wasn't feeling any pain. I think I was in shock — I'd never broken anything before — and the bones in my wrist were sticking forward, not piercing skin but there was this weird lump like I had some sort of disease.'

No-one seemed in the least alarmed. 'No ice pack, and it was just really perfunctory: well, if you want to play, that's what happens. By the time I got taken out to be driven to hospital there were about four kids left and it had all gone on oblivious. I love that about it, nothing got in the way of the bullrush. And you got the sense that every single game, someone was going to hurt themselves or break something and it just happened to be me that day.

'I don't know why I had such an enthusiasm for something that I was so bad at, but I did, because it just seemed to me exciting.' She was the kid who kept falling down and kept going. 'I think it's actually better for kids that way. You say "I got hurt and then it got better" and it's fine and you just keep going. I think today everyone's so afraid and so risk-averse and so worried about anyone getting hurt that nobody does anything.'

The 1980s and early 1990s were such a different time. Kids were falling out of trees, someone was falling through the trampoline. 'I drove my bike first time straight into a lamppost, with no helmet. You'd come off a home-made trolley down a really massive hill and scrape all of the skin off your body and it was just par for the course and expected.'

Scary things if you overcome them are really joyful things. 'It's like when you're scared to go on a roller coaster at Rainbow's End and *you're not tall enough, you're not tall enough, you're not tall enough* and eventually you are. And then you freak out and you don't go on it, you go home and feel miserable and then when you finally do go you nearly spew, but you do it. And you hate it the whole time, but you feel so elated that you've done it. It's such a weird psychology, but I think the bullrush fits into that because you always feel better for having been a part of it, even though you've broken your wrist or gotten the blood nose rather than sitting on the sidelines.'

It's the same with falling off a horse. 'The first time I thought, I'm going to die or break my neck or something, and all I did was just sort of slide off the horse and fall down. And I went oh, oh, okay, then went faster and faster and I learned to gallop and canter and ride without a saddle because I knew what the sensation of falling off would be like. It's demystifying the worst that could happen, I guess.'

She recently played laser strike for the first time in ages because she had fond memories of that and nobody was under thirty-five. 'We all ran around puffing, and the oldest person was fifty and it was just completely joyful because it was being part of a team. It's that sense of everybody being involved in doing something exciting together. When you had to play sports at school, it was just tedious. It wasn't because you wanted to, it's because you had to do a code or something like that. Those ones that you loved so much that involved terror are the ones you lean towards rather than the ones you had to do.

'If we went away camping and someone played an impromptu bullrush, I would be in straight away. It's got that rosy glow of childhood and adolescence to me, where you learned things that were a bit tough, but it was just really joyful.'

The most important thing about your school years was how good you were at bullrush.

11
Len Brown

Mayfield Primary School

1963–66

Len Brown was sharp and fast out on the wing —
'I inherited some of my father's fast physical wheels.'
But he played most of his rugby at halfback and that's
how he played his bullrush: looking for the gap, coming up through the
middle, sitting at the back end of some of the big grunters who would lead
the charge. 'I would track them through and then try and shoot the gap and
use my pace to beat the cover defenders.' He could step off both feet, he had
enough toe to explode and head off once he was through. He loved it.

He was a boy of Otara. Bullrush was a rite of passage. The most important thing about your school years was how good you were at bullrush and, secondly, how good you were at padda tennis. 'The rest of it was just cream on the cake.'

Where did they play it? 'Right in front of the school. Certainly not hiding out some back field. And on the odd occasion teachers would either participate or stand and make sure that no-one came out too bloody.'

They had fifteen minutes; they went hard. 'Otara back in the day was about sixty per cent Pakeha, forty per cent Maori, with bits and pieces of Niueans and Tongans who were the early part of the PI migration into NZ. And the Maori, they were coming from Ngati Porou or nga bush.'

You're never too young to start learning to count the votes and make allies. 'The nga bush boys were headhunters, and you stayed clear of those guys because they were really good at coat-hangering. I made sure I was in their team. Generally, they were bigger than me, and faster, but not as quick off their feet. So I would make sure I was the guy doing the pick-up and get some of the bigger, faster units in my team – then in the bullrush, I'd be tracking them through.'

There was some talent in those games. 'Hemi Wiki ended up playing second five in the Maori All Blacks and he was a very talented player. At that point he was about six inches taller than anyone else so he matured very fast, Hemi. He had a ton of toe, and you'd need it, playing second five for the Maori All Blacks. He was definitely one of those that I would track through and then just wait for the opportunities.'

'But look,' he says, 'it wasn't just blokes. It was boys and girls, whatever, anyone was in.' It was a school of about 250; almost the whole school would play. 'It was massive. You'd have two hundred kids out there, just great streams of kids piling through and looking to take out the defender. Two hundred kids just going for it, fabulous fun.'

The most memorable part — apart from running for your life — was the noise. The hollering, the yelping, the yelling, to put off the defenders. 'So that first part is a lot of racket and then secondly, of course, if you manage to escape the defenders and you're off, I mean it's like scoring a try. It's a real sense of *Yeah! And I'm off to the next round*.'

They played it all over the place, any time. Fifteen hard minutes at playtime, but if you were mucking around after school and were playing bullrush it might go on for hours, until the middle of the night in summer.

Bullrush, he says, is instinctive. You work with what you've got. 'I've talked about attack, but the second part of the game is defence. And when you're there on the receiving end and looking to take someone out, I formed an artistic expertise in the field of ankle tapping. Because I was always pretty much smaller than most of the kids, never had much height about me, and being a cheeky halfback, I would allow them to slip by me or get their way by me, but had enough pace to basically hunt most down. And if I was a little bit wary about tackling, I'd just basically clip their ankles down there.' It's a real art form, he says. He used it to pretty good effect in high school and club rugby. Perhaps he still does, a bit.

He loved the exhilaration of it, the breaking through. 'It's like a full-frontal assault on the troops in a battle.' And he likes what it taught you. How to find your way through a difficult situation, being innovative in attack and defence. 'I mean, how can I get through there — this character who's defending is massive, he's fast, what am I gonna do now?' And teamwork doesn't necessarily mean the entire group. 'Even though it's all for one and one for all, by and large you're just going for it, and the best way to operate is in teams of three, four or five, and be able to all get through against a very packed defence.'

And your enemy becomes your ally. 'Oh, as soon as you're caught, yeah. Then basically it's arm in arm and shoulders packed together and whoever's coming down, we're gonna take them out and end this game.'

It was great, says the man who has spent a lifetime dealing with statutes and by-laws. There are no rules, except for the lines on the field.

He once broke his wrist playing the game as a fifteen-year-old at De La Salle, being overly bullish about going through the middle, trying to fend someone off too directly. 'I basically bent my wrist to a point where it wouldn't bend any more, so I ended up in Middlemore. But it was a game that was very, very robust and even though there were no rules, you wouldn't get gratuitous, stupid violence. I can't remember anyone just laying someone low with a flat-out punch like that. Everyone would by and large respect the safety of others.'

No-one went too far. 'You just had to knock them over and that meant that coat-hangers and all that sort of stuff which I knew of and felt on a number of occasions in rugby games, wasn't that evident in bullrush. Mostly people came into you around your bootlaces or tackled you conventionally. Or jump on your back if they missed you or chased you down.'

As great as it was, he doesn't know if kids are missing out by being deprived of it. 'My generation, maybe the generation after, we didn't have a lot of school sport. I had a choice of two or three games. We made our own sport, and bullrush was one of them.

'I just had [sports administrator] Dave Currie in here before. A school he was at today had forty active sports. Forty. I mean, go back in my day, rugby, softball, padda tennis, gymnastics — and netball for the girls.' Schools today, the swimming, water polo, rowing, you name it, they've got it. Unbelievable choice. But they're missing out on the camaraderie and the sheer exhilaration of bullrush, aren't they? Well, maybe, he says. They were pretty great memories.

Lets plaY BuUrush

So we get pulled down

12
Midge Marsden

West End Primary School
New Plymouth

1950–57

How many people can say they got their
name from playing bullrush? Midge can.

'My real name is Keith. I was christened Keith.' In bullrush he was one of those small, running, weaving players, Keith Marsden and his little mate Peewee Clegg. 'I loved it because it was the only thing I was actually good at.'

Everyone else seemed to be a lot bigger than him. 'There was this guy, his name was Roger. He was a bigger guy than us and he was always quite aggressive. He was — what's the word? — a kind of aggro bully. Not the kind who beat people up but a bit of a heavy. And he'd laugh at us. And he was the one that named me Midget.'

It stuck. 'And second name being Marsden, I guess it just rolled off the tongue and evolved — Midget Marsden. And eventually the T got dropped.'

There was a school reunion five years ago. 'It reminds me

of that TV commercial — "One day, Roger Phipps, one day."' Roger had ended up in Australia and he turned up at the school reunion, a few marriages and a few disappointments behind him. He was looking a bit older than the rest of them, Midge thought.

'And I kinda thought, well there you go — bit of karma. Not in a nasty way, but I got up and sang a few songs at the thing and I told the story. And I think he felt quite good about it, actually. I said, "Well, Roger, I thought at the time, what are you calling me that for all the time? — but in hindsight I think you helped me advance my career something terrible."'

Bullrush was never something they just did occasionally. 'It was rampant. We did it all the time — winter, summer — it was a very popular and kind of skilful thing. You made your own fun — there were no computers or television to go home to. We always looked forward to it.'

The rules were very strictly adhered to. The bigger, older guys would make sure of it. 'They never had whistles or anything but there was always a sort of set of protocols that you adhered to — nobody cheated.'

And it was always a hell of a lot of fun. 'I could run like the wind and weave and I was really good at it. I pride myself on how good I was.' Last man over a lot? 'Yes. Not all the time, but close to it. I really sort of honed my craft.' Not so much practice at bringing them down then? He wasn't so keen on that side of it. Although: 'The big boys weren't that hard to bring down, actually. I think Peewee Clegg and I would combine our efforts to get one guy. And it was always the smaller guys that could catch the smaller guys, that could keep up and catch me, you know?'

It all stopped when they got to high school. 'We were really interested in girls and they weren't really interested in bullrush. And I started getting into music.'

He vividly remembers Danie Craven coming to the school during the 1956 Springbok tour. And he planted a tree; they all stood around and he had that green blazer with the yellow collar. 'All these memories of the time. That's one of them. And Roger naming me was the other one. Midget Marsden.'

13
Michèle A'Court

Levin North

1966–71

'Is it wrong to say that there's something quite sexy about it?' she asks. Michèle A'Court sees two things when she sees a game of bullrush: democracy, and a mating dance. She was a Trotskyite at university; these days she's more Fabian. She can analyse anything from a political point of view and when she looks at bullrush, Michèle sees democracy. Democracy and wandering hands. Boys and girls all together.

'It was one of those rare moments where boys and girls could — I think that was part of the motivation at intermediate — get their hands on each other.' Perhaps those teachers who disapproved of bullrush were worrying less about broken arms and more about groping? 'I think that it was at some sort of level a kind of mating dance. It certainly was all very visceral. It's really primal, isn't it?'

And democratic. 'I do chuck that word around quite a lot but everybody's in, everybody's equal.' It was a group activity. Everybody regardless of ability was part of the group. You weren't playing a team sport where each person in the team had a specific job; you just always played as a group. She liked that a lot.

And, she suspects, kids knew it was a bit rebellious. It was not one of the approved games. 'You know how every now and then teachers would say, "All right, everybody outside for a game of stickball," or one of those? No teacher ever said, "All right, everybody out for a game of bullrush."'

She doesn't remember the rules or the structure of the game at all. 'All I can really remember is massive excitement and thrills and this sort of glorious pack mentality that was inclusive rather than unpleasant.

'In my head I can smell cut grass, and feel the hot sun and hear people shrieking gleefully and tearing up and down a paddock and I don't know if we ever knew what the rules were or what we were doing. I think I can even hear my mother's voice saying, "Don't you go playing bullrush 'cause you'll rip your cardy."'

Injuries? Not that she can really recall, maybe a vague memory of a kid with a broken arm.

What happens when you like the look of playing sport but you're smaller than the others? Disappointment. 'I wasn't ever picked for teams because I was very small and actually I was pretty good at catching and throwing but nobody believed that. And that's one of those self-perpetuating things where you suddenly get nervous under a high ball 'cause nobody thinks you're gonna catch it so you don't.'

But bullrush can give you a chance to shine. 'I did have my little moments of stardom in it because I was a fast runner and I was a really good sidestepper but I also think I was so small that people would give me a free pass. So sometimes when I thought I was doing really well, I think people were just being kind ...'

They played it on a massive field — at least through the eyes of a school kid

— at Levin North Primary School. Intermediate only opened when she was in standard three, so when she was younger, the standard five and standard six kids were there.

'We would want to get involved but I can remember — because they were *huge* — you'd never get your name called, because they didn't know who you were. But you could be part of the bullrush.

'Word would go around school — the big kids are playing bullrush — and you would be mesmerised. So you'd go and sort of be joining in but sort of spectating.'

And there was also the possibility that some of the younger kids could shine. 'You might be ten and they might be twelve but you might be huge and so therefore you could have a shining moment like a really amazing sidestep or a full-on tackle, so it was a leveller as well.'

She was in the second intake for Levin Intermediate. 'It had just been built, and I distinctly remember playing bullrush, not on the playing field but on the grassy patch between the school and the farmland.'

A big group playing? 'Yeah, huge, huge, and all these pubescent boys and I can smell their feet from here. Feet and armpits, that's what intermediate makes me think of.'

And the girls were involved too? 'I remember it as being all of us. All in. Yeah. Levin, see, hard as nails, the ladies.'

They never saw a teacher getting involved. Bullrush wasn't banned but it wasn't sanctioned. But perhaps all the same, some of the rugby teachers might have been talent scouting from the staffroom?

'Yeah! I bet: "That one's not frightened to tackle, that one's handy on the wing. And look at her, she'd make a great ball boy. Give her a flag, go on, she's got a good eye."'

That girl will be a comedian when she gets bigger?
'Yes! But especially if she doesn't!'

14
Wallace Chapman

Manurewa East Primary School
1975–78

There was something primordial about it. It was the adrenalin of the playtime bell going and fifteen minutes to squeeze in as much bullrush as you could. You didn't need a single piece of gear or equipment. At the end of the 1970s, the action figure market was getting big, all the Star Wars stuff, 'but there wasn't much of that going down in Manurewa East'.

Wallace has been reading *Hello Girls & Boys*, Dave Veart's history of New Zealand toys. 'There was a total absence of that in the running game of bullrush. There's no Hornby train set, there's no Fun Ho! toy, there's not even knucklebones and marbles.'

He's fascinated by the notion in the book of the *wild child*. 'The early colonials, their kids, fuck, they were wild — their main plaything, both boys and girls, was a knife. You'd take your knife out into the bush, you'd carve things out, you'd make huts out of your knife, you'd whittle stuff. And the little sailing boat was *huge*, and what you had was a lot of drownings. You go to a cemetery and you see a lot of children — little Percy, eight years old, drowned; Matthew, eight, drowned — because of the absolute love of toy boats, and more often than not, unsupervised, so they'd go deeper into the lake or the river or a fast stream, these young kids. And so bullrush is a kind of historical extension of that wild child play. I mean as kids I can just remember going *fuck, this is exciting, it's great*.'

Wallace didn't duck and weave. 'No, I was terrible, I liked being the chaser, but the dodging and weaving, fuck! There was one guy, my best friend, called Arthur Pia, and he was unreal at dodging. Three of my best mates, guys called Pakira Ruhe, Arthur Pia, Steven Craike, the bullrush team. And I was that little Pakeha kid who just tried to run and keep up. It was just fun being part of it.'

The danger wasn't even a notion in their bullrush, or the fact that it might have been dangerous. He can't understand the notion of bullrush being dangerous, I mean over and above any sort of sport. Although at Manurewa East, there was no tackling. The whole challenge was to be fleet of foot, dodging and weaving. That's how you got your reputation. By great dodging and weaving.

'It was the classical us against them. So it's pitting wit against skill in a very, very simple form. You ask yourself of all the games you could have played and all the games you can play now, what was it about bullrush that was just so exciting? And it's just simply you saw the fence on the other side of the field, you saw the width of it, and that rush of actually being one of the few runners left when you're down to five, that was something else.'

No equipment, no shoes. They ran barefoot on the playing fields. Once when grass was being resown they tried it on the asphalt, 'but it didn't feel right, you know? It didn't have that malleability and that sort of let's go for it sort of style. The idea of just running from one end of the field to the other. Great memories. And the teachers were just fine; Mr Brown the principal, watching us, laughing, saying, "Ah, Arthur, you've done well."'

It wasn't a clique sport. There was one game of bullrush on the field for the school, and that was it. 'I think that made it more exciting, that challenge of having the two chasers first up and then thirty kids along the end of the field rushing.'

Perhaps the most appealing thing about bullrush was what it wasn't — the conventional sport where you pick sides. 'Later on I went to Nelson College for boys, which was pretty much the other end of the scale in terms of the demography of schooling and parents. There was a lot of picking going on for teams and I was never picked, and it kind of affected me. I think it was a combination of things. I was getting into music so I'd hang out with the music people, but I really hated team sports with a total passion because I would not get picked and so anything that was associated with a team, I really had quite a fear of. It really does affect a kid's confidence, it really does. And when you're left there with two others — Quentin and me and someone else — and it was like there's got to be another way of involving young people in sport. Bullrush inverted that because it was kids making their own play and there was an unspoken rule that no-one owned bullrush; you turn up and you get to the end of the field. It was just great.'

He went away from team sports, but for a while, before he got sick — he has a rare blood disease — he embraced long-distance running. 'I was really focused on not just the doing of it but the philosophy of it — up hills, down dale and that almost semi-meditative aspect where you come back from a long run very much being in the present. That's the only equivalent I have to what I felt after a good hour of bullrush at Manurewa East.'

He can't think of a comparable game that people feel so strongly about. Whenever you talk about it on talkback, the calls light up. 'With bullrush it was just something that at the heart of it was just really really damn good fun. You couldn't wait to play and you actually came back after lunch just totally exhilarated and totally amped. How bizarre, you know?

'I don't believe I ever spoke in a classroom from the age of five till I left at seventeen.' Rodney Hide

15
Rodney Hide

Rangiora Borough Primary School

1961–69

They played it all the time, the boys. They played it at every break, they played it after school, and they played it on the lawn at the Rangiora public swimming pool and that's the game Rodney Hide remembers most vividly. 'We were playing in our togs, and I can remember pushing my very good friend Jimmy Thompson into the fence to slow him down and it was a big cyclone fence and he caught his upper arm and his shoulder and this big chunk of meat came out like you wouldn't believe. Fuck, it was a mess.'

School mostly was a huge disappointment to him. It was mechanical, it wasn't taught to interest you. 'Look, I never spoke — no-one believes this — I don't believe I ever spoke in a classroom from the age of five till I left at seventeen. I never spoke, no-one asked me anything, I never said anything. You just sat there like a receptacle. And it was mind-numbingly boring for a kid.'

He goes to schools today and it's fantastic, what they do, so different to his experience. 'It seemed to me that what it was doing for us was preparing us literally in the Prussian style, to be ready for the freezing works, where they rang the bell and you went to work and they rang the bell and you stopped.'

But bullrush, or Bar the Door as they called it in Rangiora, well, that was brilliant. 'I can remember it being extremely exhilarating and just so exciting. You couldn't wait to get out there; you'd have mud all down your leg from fighting in the grass. We'd basically run until you could hardly stand up and then you'd go and sleep in class, ready for having another crack after school.'

Rugby by comparison was a bit tame, what with the rules and a ref. Bullrush was a complete free-for-all, 'and I'm amazed, apart from Jimmy Thompson

I can't remember anyone being hurt'.

There was honour to it. People think of it as very physical, but in fact no-one wanted to hurt the other guy. 'I was mortified that I'd hurt Jimmy Thompson and it's etched on my brain.'

He can't ever remember anyone wanting to hurt someone. The big kids didn't know the little kids, but they wouldn't throw them across from one end of the field to the other. 'I distinctly remember big guys gently picking me up and saying you're out and laying me down ever so gently. And then when you were in standard six you would have fun with little kids doing the same.

'And a great thing about the game is this: you'd graduate each year. So you started playing standard two or whatever and you end up a standard six kid, so your role changes. Every year you're a bigger kid, you're a bigger kid, and you're still playing the game.

'Little kids would turn up and they'd go weaving down the field giggling away and these big Maori kids would be picking them up and gently putting them down.'

He doesn't know if that still holds today. There are kids who want to hurt other kids. And there's a disparity in size. 'You know, you see kids at high school now and even primary school, they're monsters. Not just fat, I mean tall. I've watched it casually in high school rugby matches and there are Jonah Lomu types and you're thinking *Jesus* — we just didn't have that.'

He was never a duck-and-weave guy. 'Sadly, given my physique — little legs and stocky — I tended to be head down, push my way through, and I was hooker at rugby and so I was head down, keep going and don't stop.'

But it equipped him for life, for politics. It didn't matter how big they were, if you hit them hard enough, you could get through.

He has never doubted that he would get through. He could do this. Whatever it was. He always fronted up in bullrush, telling himself with absolute conviction he was Charlie Upham or someone in Crete and he would just bust through. He never would stop.

And nine times out of ten he'd get dragged down. 'But you'd get up this next time and you were going to get through. And again that was what was great about it — it was so fast; rugby was slow by comparison. And of course you never had a down moment because you were always running — up and down or trying to catch the other fella. So in ten minutes, a lot of action would happen.'

There were the dissections, afterwards, of who did what when: 'Oh bloody Johnny, you know, did you see, three guys, two hanging on his legs and he was still going, you know. Legend!'

The other thing about that game is that it wasn't necessarily the big guys who were good at it. 'A little guy getting around your neck or getting around your legs or getting around a shoulder, it all counted, didn't it? I can remember big guys going down the field with two or three kids hanging off them and slowing them down sufficiently for a big guy to catch up and drop him. Everyone had a part to play. So the wee fast guy would take off and jump on a guy's back and hang on for dear life and then another kid would jump on and then some lumbering big kid would come up and just push him over. That's a great metaphor for life.

'The big guy who was the captain of the first fifteen, he would never get called. He was the last one caught. He'd just sort of lope down from one end to the other until there was enough on side that they could drag him down. So it was the little guy getting through at the first go that would get all the cheers.'

He believes in the power of the market, he admires the way it allows for endless experimentation. His great motivation in politics was to stop the government from stymieing that.

He sees a metaphor for that in bullrush: no rules, no referee, no-one got hurt, everyone had a part to play. 'And the funny thing is, and this is the great economics thing — you'd think if you were the little guy you'd just get smashed to bits, but the little guy, he helped at the start because he was the first guy through. And the little guy would help you bring down a big guy. So that's a perfect metaphor — because in a market economy there's a role for everyone.

'You look at a game of rugby now and I defy anyone to know what the rules are now. These games that we played as kids are now so tied up in the rules and yet we played games that had no rules and they were fun to play and everyone sort of understood an unwritten rule. But I can't imagine school kids following the line-out rule, all those rules about offside. I watch a game of rugby now and I don't know what they're blowing the whistle about. As kids, we didn't have that, did we?'

He learned to swim at the school pool in Cust. He went back there nearly half a century later with his young daughters and it all felt as fresh in his memory as yesterday. He used to love jumping off the diving board, again and again: 'I'd go running along, jump off the diving board and wait to be rescued and you know, a sister or a cousin would fish me out. I'd just go straight to the bottom. Isn't that a hoot? Well, my kids are the same. I take my girls swimming — they're three and two; they like nothing better than jumping in from the side and being rescued and they'll sink like a stone and you'll fish them out and in they jump again. It never occurs to them that they won't be fished out, and to be fair, it never occurs to me not to.

'And I can remember people complaining, "Jesus, you know, haven't you had enough?" And I'd laugh and I'd go running back onto the board and in I'd jump again, and cousin John would jump in again and fish me out.'

There's no such thing as a failed experiment. He explains to people that most of his life he's been wrong, 'but that's how you learn, isn't it? I'm never hard particularly on people, because I try not to be, because I'm wrong about everything I know.'

16
Brendhan Lovegrove

Dilworth School
1980–88

When Brendhan Lovegrove first played bullrush, he was the trophy. 'I had an older brother Daryl there and he was very popular, so to take out the younger brother of one of the seniors at the school was of huge interest. It was "That's Lovegrove's brother, let's get him". So I was always first to go. And it was always highly embarrassing to be taken down by the younger brother of one of the seniors so it was also high credibility if I was able to bring down one of the older boys.'

Boys will be boys. It could get a little bit rough. There would be fights. That would stop the game. 'And then it would be just a semicircle around two guys bashing the shit out of each other until a prefect was told to go away or a teacher would barge his way through and they would take you to the headmaster's office and caned, at least three each.'

Dilworth in that era could be severe. You could be caned for getting mud on your shoes. You could be caned for getting mud on your socks. You could be caned for getting mud on anything. 'It wasn't totally out of the realms of possibility that a good thirty or forty boys could be lined up and just whacked for breaking the rules.

'Caning was weird. Today it would just be out-and-out assault; in the eighties it was just what you did to kids. You lay a hand on them these days and you get in trouble. But it was a particularly bad thing to do at a lot of boarding schools because a lot of the people permitted to cane were university students working there as tutors. So if they had a problem with a kid they could just bend them over and whack them. It was legalised assault in a way. And it bloody hurt.

'Our generation seriously had some philosophical and difficult problems. But then we were also much more call a spade a spade. Today it's ridiculous. I find the world very PC.'

Bullrush was huge at Dilworth, the staple diet for fun at lunchtime. It was the one thing the young kids could do together with the older boys. Everyone — virtually the whole school — would be on the field, great for a young kid who wanted to be noticed. If you wanted to impress, you found a way. But the last man standing was always a first fifteen member. 'Always. Or a real sneaky fast dude. One of your sprinters who no-one could lay a finger on.'

Bullrush is extremely confronting. 'You're running and suddenly you've got this bloody big person coming towards you and it's quite real because their only intent is to stop you. In a moment of time it's quite an intimidating prospect. Your heart beats boom boom and you go *I've gotta get away from this*. And the next thing you know you could be down on the ground going, "Ohhh Christ." And then there's some guy going, "There you go, mate. You're all good." And then you're doing it.

'Or some big guy comes towards you and you might decide to just let them go — "Have a good time, on you go." Or you go, "No, I'm going to do this."

'And for a small short time it's going to be very intense but possibly also painful. It's quite a moment. You know you're running but at that moment of time because of its intensity it's also a pretty interesting life experience.'

He doesn't think anyone really got hurt. 'It's very difficult to be hurt at bullrush. I don't think anyone goes in there to do a full-on head-high tackle. People are just trying to get you down.'

You can't cheat at bullrush. If you get tackled, you're gone. 'You don't want to be the one that's thinking, "Oh no, I'm going to run to the other side." There's none of that because somebody will go, "Hey!" and a lot of people will go, "No, I've tackled you." So there was no cheating.

'I still remember the days where there was that last dude and just heaps of guys going right and they would do it because they were just that big or that fast. They were the true athletes. It really didn't matter who was in front of them or is in front of them, it was like watching John Kirwan in the eighties.'

Dilworth is a school for boys without parents or with single parents. 'We started at eight years old at Dilworth and finished at seventh form, so we were very young and very old all playing and obviously all the eight- and nine-year-olds were out very quickly, but it was all very respectfully done and no-one was hurt. It was great and it was an everyday occurrence. What a great thing to do, in a beautiful surrounding. Made for childhood in many ways. It's a perfect memory.'

'All you've got to do is run and don't get caught.'

Frank Bunce

17
Frank Bunce

Mangere

1967–74

'All you have to do is mention bullrush and you've got bloody fifty friends,' says Frank Bunce, legend.

'He played a lot of bullrush? Well, that figures,' says Brendhan Lovegrove, rugby fan. 'He had such an amazing fend, Frank Bunce. What a great centre. He wasn't all about just smashing through the middle. He would have a bit of a sidestep and when he got through it was because of pace and a really good fend. You don't just fend people off because you're big and you've got a big arm. A fend is a skill. A skill you can get from bullrush.'

Growing up in Mangere, they played it a little bit at school, lunchtime, but you'd end up going inside with your clothes ripped and all sweaty and bruised and battered sometimes, so you didn't do too much of that. And you'd get told off by the teacher, then get home and maybe get told off again, maybe get a whack across the ear because you ripped whatever you were wearing.

But at weekends, it was huge. Those games went on for hours and hours and hours, just a group of the neighbourhood kids who might happen to be there. All ages, definitely all ages, and it was both guys and girls. It would turn into hour upon hour; it could go a whole day, in fact. You'd get tired, so you'd have breaks, and start again. It just rolled on. Eventually you might get hungry or get called home and that was pretty much it. Or you'd just play until you didn't want to any more. You just wandered off.

He liked it so much, he exported it to Italy. How long does it take to teach people bullrush in Italy? About a minute, Frank says. 'They caught on right away. All you've got to do is run and don't get caught.'

A friend of his was coaching there. 'He'd played for the club when he was a young fella and then had gone away and done his thing; I played for Samoa with him at the World Cup in 1991. He actually went on to coach Italy itself. Anyway, he was coaching this club and I was up there with TV3, I think it was, at the time, and he asked me if I was interested in helping out. I thought it would be quite fun.'

It was a little place called Rovato. They were doing the usual stuff with training. But it can get really, really cold up there. Much of the time you can't train outside, certainly not in the middle of winter.

'We had them in the school gyms and things like that. For a bit of a change we put them through the jungle gyms and that kind of thing. A little add-on. None of them had ever swung on ropes or climbed and played on the jungle gyms and all that sort of stuff.'

They were just looking for little games to play at training, different things for warm-ups. 'I can't even remember how it came up but we just said, "Let's play bullrush." They'd never heard of it. Never played it. They just didn't do that sort of stuff when they were growing up. So we used bullrush as a warm-up drill.'

It taught them valuable skills: evasion and tackling, 'a whole pile of things. It's sidestepping, it's dodging, it's swerving, it's all of that sort of stuff and you learn it in an instant, really. They loved it — that was the great part about it. Every time you wanted to play bullrush, it was just a quick setup and everyone was in.'

They ranged from age nineteen to mid-thirties, maybe forty of them playing two squads as a warm-up. It was a powerful game. The small ones would use their pace and their sidestep, the big ones would just try to go straight up the middle. It was fun rather than work. 'And that was always the reason for doing it, because it's not as if it was organised, it was *let's have some fun*.'

18
Christine Rose

Kaipara College
1983–87

Christine Rose has a photo from the final day of her sixth form year at Kaipara College. It's after exams. That wonderful liberated summer feeling of end of exams. A day you're feeling as exuberant as that, you play bullrush. There are thirty or so of them, being nostalgic at the end of their school life about the game they had played so many times.

Kaipara College is a rural school. A lot of them would arrive as much as an hour and a half before class. They played bullrush while they waited. 'That's the great thing about it — you could adapt any bit of ground. It didn't need to be flat, it could be big or small.'

She can remember only one person ever getting hurt in all those years. 'We were playing on a bank and somebody was doing a skid along the ground and they hit a hidden tap without a top on it. So that was my first look at the inside of somebody's leg. But that wasn't from the bullrush per se, anybody could have encountered that. Pretty nasty though.'

The older boys were rugby players and they took it a lot more seriously. 'We were a little bit more discretionary — almost cannon fodder — the little girls, so almost superfluous to the game but that's the nature of bullrush, that it's not elite and so it was all comers and even those little pawns of us who weren't big and brawny, we still had a role to play.'

Sometimes you had to be pretty brave to run in and face solid burly people. You gave it your best shot, ran like hell as far as you could, did your manoeuvring, but if they got you, you had the option of crumpling. 'You didn't have to come to your opposition chest-on. I seem to recall that that was a strategy of mine — I'll just collapse here.'

It wasn't so much about winning or losing. When it came to bullrush, even though there was a sort of pseudo aggression, it was always in the sense of fun.

It's not like the team contest we're so used to. It's fluid. It's being with just about everybody on the same team, halfway through it's half and half, and then at the

end everybody's on the other team that they started from. You get constantly changing allegiances, depending on how many people and where you are in those arrays. 'In a sense, at the end everybody wins.'

We see games as fierce and divided. We see life that way too. 'Everything's winners and losers, you're either good or you're not. Bullrush challenges that way of seeing things. It allows you to see and accept and actually embrace the fact that we might be on one side to start with but in minutes we're going to be on the other side. Loyalties change — as soon as you're tagged, you're one of them.

'Here's a game that actually does allow some sort of transcending of the normal rules of the game, of winning and losing, and yet it was condemned because it was too violent. So what sort of subtext is going on there? They actually don't like us being able to step into other shoes — it looks subversive! We're going to stop this — too many people empathising and cooperating. Ban that!'

19
Jacinda Ardern

David Street Primary School, Morrinsville

1985–91

'It's funny, when I think about it I can't quite decipher between my memories of playing the actual game and my nightmares of playing it. I think some of it was a dream and some of it was real. The outcome was generally the same.'

She remembers primary school as a place of bumps and bruises. 'I was quite a clumsy child but reasonably fearless as well. I used to climb trees a lot — and I remember at least one occasion losing my footing up a large tree on the back field and hooking my underwear onto a branch and literally swinging from my underpants, which unfortunately gave way. So I had to wear my togs around school for the rest of the day. They said "Mum's number one" on the front of them as well. That was not a nightmare. That actually happened.'

Bullrush was the least of her concerns, really. 'Bullrush at least was a group activity as opposed to me humiliating myself on an individual level.'

Jacinda doesn't think the teachers were particularly concerned about bullrush. If they were concerned about hazards they probably would have got rid of the massive maypole at the back of the field, on the side of a hill. Three ropes dangling off it with knots on the bottom and if you got a good speed up, ran around and grabbed the knot you'd be airborne. 'I gave myself a lot of injuries on the poorly sealed netball courts — I played netball as a primary school kid and we didn't have proper ankle support, you know, just plain flat sandshoes. I sprained my ankle about three times playing netball until they were pretty much toast. We never did stretching — it was just out there and straight into it.'

Her most vivid primary school memory by far is the Edgecumbe earthquake. 'There were primers in the swimming pool — so we all just ran to the windows to watch the primers get sloshed around. That is my enduring memory of the Edgecumbe earthquake. Dog eat dog, that's what primary school is. I definitely remember it being a good shake. My teacher, Miss Maude, was holding this heavy-duty boombox and dropped it as soon as the earth started shaking. Just froze. While we all ran for cover.'

So she was no use? 'No. No use. But she didn't stop us watching the primers, so that was good.'

You don't know until it happens whether you'll be fight, flight or paralysis. It's entirely instinctual. In that moment, the strong people emerge. 'That's right. They're probably the ones who will be good at bullrush.'

How did she play her bullrush? 'Definitely duck-and-weave. I always had this little sense of hesitation. Hesitation, then close your eyes, then duck-and-weave. Maybe fearless isn't the right word; I probably wrongfully calculated danger. Bullrush I probably did view with quite a lot of trepidation. That was a known risk. I could see it, it was in front of me, it was usually bigger.'

She tweeted once about having drawn on her bullrush skills in the course of her job. 'Someone thought that I wasn't in parliament because they hadn't seen me that day and it was actually because I had done a swifty little duck-and-weave around the crews and gone up the back stairs. It's definitely a skill I've come to appreciate.'

She reflects for a moment. Actually, the skill of just charging would probably work for you just as well. That would be the Judith Collins approach? 'Yes. Slightly less skill.'

20
Greg McGee

Oamaru North School

1955–62

In standard three and four, rugby was played according to weight. Tall and gangly Greg McGee, a little bit heavier, would get put in with the older boys. 'The fat and the blind.'

They were useless. 'I'd be standing there at first five eighths crying, *literally crying*, with frustration, tears running down my cheeks, how bad they were.'

But bullrush, that was a whole lot better. You got to play with the kids your own age and not be forever losing. It felt good. You actually had successes. You realised you were actually quite handy. You didn't play it in boots, you played in bare feet and it was wonderful.

'It's sort of quite primal, isn't it? You're running with the herd trying not to be picked out.'

Sometimes it was a race and the slowest were in the middle, but other times it was reversed and you would be in the middle, eyeing the herd like a predator thinking, *I'll get a couple of fat slow guys* — and build up from that until you were ready to target someone who'd be really useful in the middle.

You looked forward to getting to school to play bullrush and endured the rest of it. 'I think the teachers realised that their chance of having us sit in class and pay attention depended to some extent on how much energy we were able to get rid of at playtime and lunchtime.

'There was such an exuberance to it. So unstructured. No administrators, no-one saying you couldn't play if you were this weight or you didn't wear this or that or turn up at such and such a time.' You did have to be careful about ripping shirts, though. No-one had any money.

'Bullrush is so elemental. There's no ball, there's no nothing. And there's something about being either the hunter or the hunted, trying to pick out a weak member of the herd — it's sort of going back to the plains. And it was thrilling — skating through again unnoticed, to safety.'

In some ways you had a lot more licence to try things than in formalised rugby. He wonders if the skills of some of our big guys coming through rugby were first tried out in bullrush. 'I was a big guy and I was always destined for the forwards. I couldn't step but I learned I had a body swerve, and I had speed and those things that I wouldn't necessarily have been able to perfect on the rugby field.'

There was a fairness to it. They'd have pick-up games of rugby in the park. There were a couple of older kids they played with. 'One of them dumped me really hard and hurt me and was immediately remonstrated with by the rest of the players — "Hey, that's not on!" And you couldn't just carry on winning, winning, winning. It wasn't just rampant egos and showing off.'

What about injuries? He never got hurt in bullrush, never saw it happen. He got concussed the first time when he was eight. But that was playing rugby.

High school could be brutal. Theirs was one of the last to outlaw fagging. 'There was a lot of that still around. It got passed on; you were bullied, so you bullied. It wasn't terribly enlightened. But it's interesting the difference — I remember bullrush being played at primary school and the sort of collegial atmosphere of excitement and I remember kids being looked after.

'Sometimes I think the professional game is more inclusive, funnily enough, than the amateur game was because it's all of the ability — doesn't matter what you look like, how long your hair is. But other times it's fucking frightening. The collisions and the hits. Jesus.'

He recalls the playwright David Geary touring schools for a drama initiative. He would ask the kids — fifth formers — for a show of hands: How many were looking to make a career in professional rugby or league? In places like Flaxmere, fully eighty per cent of the boys would stick their hands up, 'which is sort of alarming because that sort of career is about as fragile as your knee joint.

'I'm sixty-four and I have to manage my bones and joints and everything carefully. And I retired at twenty-three, twenty-four. But you look at the punishment someone like Richie McCaw has gone through. At one stage I told him, "One thing you don't know yet, Richie, bones have memories. All those hits — they remember." Hopefully they make a lot of money for their old age.

'But the other thing that I think it taught you that certainly applies in rugby — if you do the wrong thing, but you do it hard enough and with enough conviction, it usually turns out to be the right thing. That doesn't translate to many other sports, but it was true of bullrush: if you did whatever you were doing with enough conviction, hard enough, you were probably going to be okay.'

21
Robert Kelly

Wellington

1996–2007

Robert went to a boys' prep school, played bullrush, got his head split open. 'I never lived in a period where bullrush was allowed. But it was certainly something that we knew about.'

The school has three fields. There's a big one at the bottom, then one at the back that the junior kids played on and one behind a line of trees slightly further away from the school. In year seven and year eight that's where they'd go to play bullrush, because you had a decent line of sight. If a teacher was coming, you could turn it into touch rugby. They were allowed to play touch bullrush in that sanitised way.

Oral history had kept it alive. Brothers, older students, 'and gap students who would come over from England, it was part of their thing too'.

There was a wire fence down the side of the field, eight poles every couple of metres. They were playing bullrush, keeping a lookout. 'I wasn't a particularly big or fast kid but I was quite cunning and I thought I'd cut around the back of this guy and cut through and he managed to grab me by the shirt and swing me around.' And that's how he went head first into a pole. 'It was a real piece of bad luck because anywhere else on the fence it would have hurt a little bit but it would have been fine.'

Suddenly, there was blood everywhere. It was all go. 'At the time I was reading a bunch of young adult books that had the idea that if you weren't going to get someone else in trouble, you said you fell down the stairs, so this idea of young adult morality from the Middle Ages was in the front of my head and so I said that I'd run into a wall, and I was taken to the doctor. It must have been really obvious that I hadn't run into a wall. It was such a specific injury, but I was never called up on it and it was just kind of left. And I remember thinking at the time that that was interesting.'

But there was another level to the lie as well. 'My mum was very worried about these kind of things as well but my dad was from mid-Canterbury and kind of into this stuff. So I got home and I told Mum that I'd run into a wall. That was my story and I was sticking to it, and I don't think that she particularly bought it either but didn't question it. And I was talking to Dad, who was away overseas, and I said, "Oh, don't tell Mum but I was playing bullrush," like it was some kind of badge of honour, like I'd somehow escaped.'

Robert was eleven. 'Of course, Dad would have told Mum. But she never brought it up. So there was this weird expectation of what the game is and what it isn't.' The massive injustice of all this, as far as Robert was concerned, was that he had managed to split his head open on the day of the annual picnic. The great tradition of the picnic was to go wharf jumping, and he couldn't, 'because I had stitches in my head and even to this day I have a very rigid line of scar kind of under my hair that will be there forever'.

He never played it again.

High school began with a bullrush game, on day three, for third formers and seventh formers, which lasted twenty to twenty-five minutes. The PE teachers came running and scattered everyone away.

It happened again the next week — 'Oh, sir, we're playing touch,' and then someone would turn around and then click fingers, it would be on again. 'So it stuck around. But I remember that by the time I was in seventh form, in 2007, it had gone.'

22
Scotty Morrison

Rotorua Primary School
1976–81

It was a different time, back then. They played at interval, they played at lunchtime, they played at little playtime — a five- to ten-minute break in the afternoon, just enough time for a fast and furious game. 'But one time we were so involved and focused on the game that we didn't hear the bell and we were still out there ten minutes later, and when we headed back to class the principal was waiting for us.'

He marched about twenty-five of them down to the office, and strapped the lot for being late back to class.

'I remember the first one that got strapped we were all like *oh my goodness*.' They knew how it worked. You put your hand out and you braced yourself. The principal lifted the strap high, and brought it down with *great vengeance and furious anger* on the first kid. 'And his hand just about flew behind him and out the other side he hit him so hard. Oh my God, I think some of us were even crying before we got strapped.' Scotty was near the end of the line. It was a long wait. 'I think he was getting softer and softer by then, he was probably getting tired. I was thinking, *Oh my God, this is going to be the worst pain I'm ever going to feel*. And then he did it. And it wasn't too bad. "Put your other hand out." "Oh yes, sir." And we all went back to class.'

They had a bit of a pack mentality in their bullrush. You ran as a pack, you defended as a pack. If you were in the middle you'd have a little hui — 'So who shall we get?' And then you hunted your target as a pack. Or if there was a bullrush you'd target one person and monster them. 'You're all running at James, who is in the middle — there might be five in the middle by then so you say, "We'll all run at James, the whole lot of us, that'll increase our chances of getting through.'"

Or you lit out on your own. 'I was fortunate enough to be blessed with speed, so I just always picked out the slower people in the middle and ran for them.'

They also did a bit of base stealing, a bit of anticipation. So they'd watch the bull who was running — the kid whose name had been called. If they'd got through the middle, even if they hadn't yet made the end, you'd start your run straight away. Those kids in the middle won't be ready yet, and you might just sneak past them before they even notice you've started your run.

In bullrush, the rules, simple as they were, would get stretched a lot. Sometimes if you took off early, it would get a bit chaotic and there was really nothing those kids in the middle could do about it.

'Yeah, it was pretty loose. But sometimes you'd get a bull in the middle and they just couldn't catch anybody — it would just be a free-for-all. You'd play for an hour just running past that one person. That might have been a bit cruel. But watching the kids today I was watching them play tag — and our son did the

'We were out there all the time when it was raining.' Scotty Morrison

same thing. As soon as one of them broke through they still had a good twenty metres to run before they got to the safety zone, but off he went. Took off. Ran along the left-hand side of the field, got right across, through before the boys in the middle had turned around.'

Players could get a bit pissed off if they got caught. 'I probably would've been one of those if I had got caught.' In Ohinemutu in Rotorua their cousins lived next door to a vacant tennis court. They'd go over there for a game. 'I remember one of my cousins getting really angry when he got caught. He threw a wobbly and had a tantrum for a while and that sort of ended the game really. There were always tears in bullrush, because of an injury or because they got caught or because they got picked at some certain stage.'

But it was almost impossible to get through if you were the last runner. The whole playing area would be covered with players. 'So if you could get through, that was a pretty major achievement. Kinda felt proud of yourself for the whole day. You did get a bit of mana if you were good at it. It enhanced your mana a bit around the school ground if you were a gun bullrush player.'

Was Scotty that man sometimes? 'Well, like I said I just happened to be the fastest kid in our school — I was fortunate. And before that my brother was too, so he used to clean up at bullrush. Quite often I was the last to run. But that's because I had some speed back then. I was faster than everybody else and had a huge advantage.'

There was a lot of skill being acquired in those mad dashes. 'Having agility, picking your moments, all that sort of stuff. Even strategising — where you would run, when you would run, how you are going to get through, and then how you dealt with the pressure of trying to get through, and then the fear as well of getting caught. All those things were playing on your mind — can you play bullrush? — but you don't realise it because you're too young, you're just there for the fun of it.'

How did their shirts hold up? Not well. A lot of them just grabbed. They'd hardly ever make a decent tackle. There was no get your head behind the hips and wrap your arms around the legs. That very rarely happened. 'It was more like someone would run at you, you'd just stick your hand out and grab hold of the clothes and hold on for dear life, then wait for everybody else to come in and jump on top of the person and eventually they succumbed and fell down.'

A lot of ripped clothes, a lot of dirty clothes. They played when it was fine, they played when it was pouring down with rain. They were quite flexible, the teachers back then; if we wanted to play in the rain, so be it, off we went. 'Actually it adds to it a bit, the wetness. We played rugby league in the backyard at home a lot. Our next-door neighbour used to come over and we would play two on two outside and the best times were when it was absolutely hosing down. That would be our cue — *righto, we're going outside to play league*. I don't know if it was the atmosphere or something — the buzz of sliding around and getting wet, we just loved it. So we were out there all the time when it was raining.

'I did it with my son one time in the middle of a storm — he would have been about six. I said to him, "Get your rugby gear on, we're going outside to play league." He goes, "What?" Ten minutes. It was choice. We were sliding around in the puddles having great fun.'

Some of their more memorable bullrush games were in the wet. Everyone walked back into class absolutely drenched. 'In Rotorua you've got the geothermal stuff — we have these big panel heaters going right across the rooms; everyone would take their shirts off and hang them on the panel heaters. Sit next to that and warm up. Good times. Good times.

'I always feel quite fortunate to have grown up in the seventies and eighties. It was a fantastic time to grow up — good music and a lot safer than it is now. We grew up by Lake Rotorua and me and my older brother and our next-door neighbour, we used to have these polystyrene surfboards. We used to make some sandwiches, chuck them on the front of the surfboard, paddle off for the whole day down the stream, which was like about a kilometre away. We played the whole day until dark and then paddled back and no worries. Nothing was going to happen, we weren't going to drown, weren't going to get kidnapped or abused or something down there. It just didn't seem to come into people's thinking back then. Whereas nowadays you wouldn't let them out of your sight. Different times.'

23
Stacey Morrison

Aranui High School

1981–86

'I remember bullrush more from high school than primary because it was more traumatic. The whole ground would shake. Really big, big boys and it was like legalised fighting. It was kind of no holds barred in bullrush — that's when things got testy, when someone did something like a shoulder-barge.'

Stacey was watching her kids play bullrush — their school plays bullrush tag — 'and it's still the same, there are still those matters of contention — "I tagged you," "No, you didn't."'

If there were things to be sorted out, bullrush was a way to do it. 'It's definitely a mana-munching thing. You get some mana when you're good at bullrush.' At high school it was really only the toughest of girls who would give that a good go. Only the really tough or fast ones would go for it. And you would only have a few days of bravery. 'Or you might play until it got too scary and then you said, "Oh, I've gotta go, I've gotta go do something."'

In primary school it was the big game in the playground so to be part of it, you either were the girl who walked around watching it or you had to get involved, occasionally at least. 'It wasn't something where I went hey, that looks good, I really want to do that. But then the challenge of it was quite intriguing as well. Sometimes it would escalate and you'd go okay, oooookay, no, not my thing.'

People got hurt. Standard procedure. Sometimes blood. At primary school the ground was really hard — when you had those Christchurch nor'wester days.

'I remember a broken arm, and the poor kid trying not to cry.

'You know you always remember the fastest kid in school? That was Greg Robertson and he always came into classes with his jersey ripped and big scratches across his knees and quite a bloody lip.'

Stacey was fairly sporty, she got amongst things and was active but didn't go into formal sport very much. 'Logistically it was just very hard for my mum — single mum — to get around a lot.'

She played a tactical game. She had to. 'I've never been a big person. I played senior women's rugby in my twenties and it was the same thing then — more about speed than size.'

When she started working at TV a work friend said she was going to play rugby. 'She was about my size and I said, "Oh my God, what about if you get hurt? She said, "My mum's lived her life thinking what if and I'm not going to."

'I was always the smallest and I would lie about my weight to make it heavier. Which is unusual for a woman, I suppose.' She played amongst Black Ferns players, basically everyone in the club. First game she ever played, though, they lost by eighty points. 'It was so embarrassing. We got smashed.' All Blacks Glen Osborne and Eric Rush were there. 'They just laughed at us and said, "You were still trying to charge down the conversions." I said that was the only small piece of pride we had left. You have to keep trying.

'I guess that's how I got to understand about how men feel about combative sports — because you go into battle together. If women don't have that experience, they can be like *why are they so weird about their rugby team?* I know now it's because of the camaraderie of every week actually putting yourself in physical danger and physical dependence on the people that you're playing with. In netball you can have a good game, but no-one is likely to get smashed — it's just a different level of combat. And that's what was addictive.

'I try not to be a helicopter parent. But it's hard watching my son play league for the first time. But playing rugby and growing up in the environment I did, I sort of get it — it's a thing. I do understand testosterone outlet and the thrill. A game is never as thrilling if there isn't so much invested in it. And actually the danger adds to the excitement. That spectre of danger is part of the attraction.'

'Big kids are always going to come through holes and little kids are going to tackle them. It's just how it works.'

Josh Kronfeld

24
Josh Kronfeld

Raureka School, Hastings
1976–82

Bullrush is rugby without a ball, Josh Kronfeld says. 'There were always tears and the occasional blood but I never remember anything getting broken. I can remember the big kids getting scragged with about ten kids all hanging off them and trying to drag this guy to the ground. I just think it's a fabulous game.'

It would be the whole school playing — a single rugby field and a hundred-odd kids. The big kids never had an issue with you playing. You just had to handle it. 'It was pretty open slather.'

He was the kind of kid who was always making it a bit harder for himself. 'As they were picking up teams I'd do a scan and say, well, that's the better team — you could work that stuff out pretty quick — and I would try to go in the worst team. Just to try and even things up to really challenge myself.'

He's forty-three now and he doesn't think bullrush really exists in kids' vocabulary any more. 'They don't play the game, and we just played it all the time.' In bullrush, you honed your rugby skills: the evasion, the tackling. 'I get quite frustrated with the concept of KiwiSport in rugby. And then they dumb it down with Ripper Rugby — I understand their process for it, but kids don't get hurt at that age. They don't have the back injuries. You get the rare occasion of head on head but that can happen in Ripper as well. But at that age group they're just so bendy. I notice kids come out of Ripper, they tackle with their fingers. Their arms are long and they're trying to tackle with their hands out, and there's no shoulder involved at all. It's a foreign concept for them and they're worried about their heads because they've never had knocks in and around the face area. So they spend their whole time with their hands in front of them just trying to tackle that way. If they had bullrush, they'd be miles ahead.

'Big kids are always going to come through holes and little kids are going to tackle them. It's just how it works. If you think back to when you played it, the big kids tended to not be very lateral — they couldn't run and step as much as the other kids, so they'd run straight ahead and typically they'd pick the weakest person they could run over. So for that kid he's got a great opportunity to drop his shoulder and knock that guy over. You wouldn't get that exposure with Ripper Rugby. It doesn't happen.'

He was at uni when he first heard about schools banning bullrush. 'I was stunned. I thought it was the biggest joke I'd ever heard. I remember them saying it was for kids' welfare, but it was also uniforms — parents getting upset about uniforms getting trashed, and I do remember my mum fixing my uniforms, me coming home and I'd have a pocket torn off or a shirt ripped and she'd go, *What?* But she'd say, "You've just got to use your brain and have another shirt you can put on," or something like that.

'Look, I just think it's a travesty. Like having a white line drawn on a tree — that's as high as you can climb. I'll go to a school to give a talk and I'll ask, "What are those white lines on the tree?" and they will say, "Oh, I can't climb past that, sir."'

Let the kids work it out for themselves, he says: 'If you can climb a tree to a certain height, don't fall out of the tree — that's the first rule. The second rule is you don't climb past where you're comfortable. And the third rule is you don't climb the tree if you're not going to be able to climb it. Putting a line up there is just the dumbest shit I've ever heard of.'

He'll tell his boys: 'Hey look, you can climb up there but just be aware you can fall off.' Or: 'Take your time.' 'So I sell it that way and then I'll go and stand under if they feel uncomfortable and catch them.' They've had a couple of catches.

'If I've learned anything with my boys — and I'm still feeling my way through it — they learn better from themselves than they do from you. Something that they've done themselves, that skill becomes far more ingrained and solid than anything you do to try and show them.'

They go down to the park and he sits down and lets them go. 'I might say, "Hey, man, you're on the edge of this, it's pretty dangerous, be careful," but then you'll have the mums there and it's such a different way of caregiving. They're in there, they're following them around there: "You can't climb that, it's too high" — whereas I'll show my kids how to climb. I'll say, "You put your foot here, you put your hand here" and I'll help them learn it all, because they're going to do it when Mum's not looking. When Mum's not looking you want them to have practised and be comfortable to get to where they've got to get to. But that's my opinion.

'You can go through a lot of today's things that just don't add up, in my head,' he says.

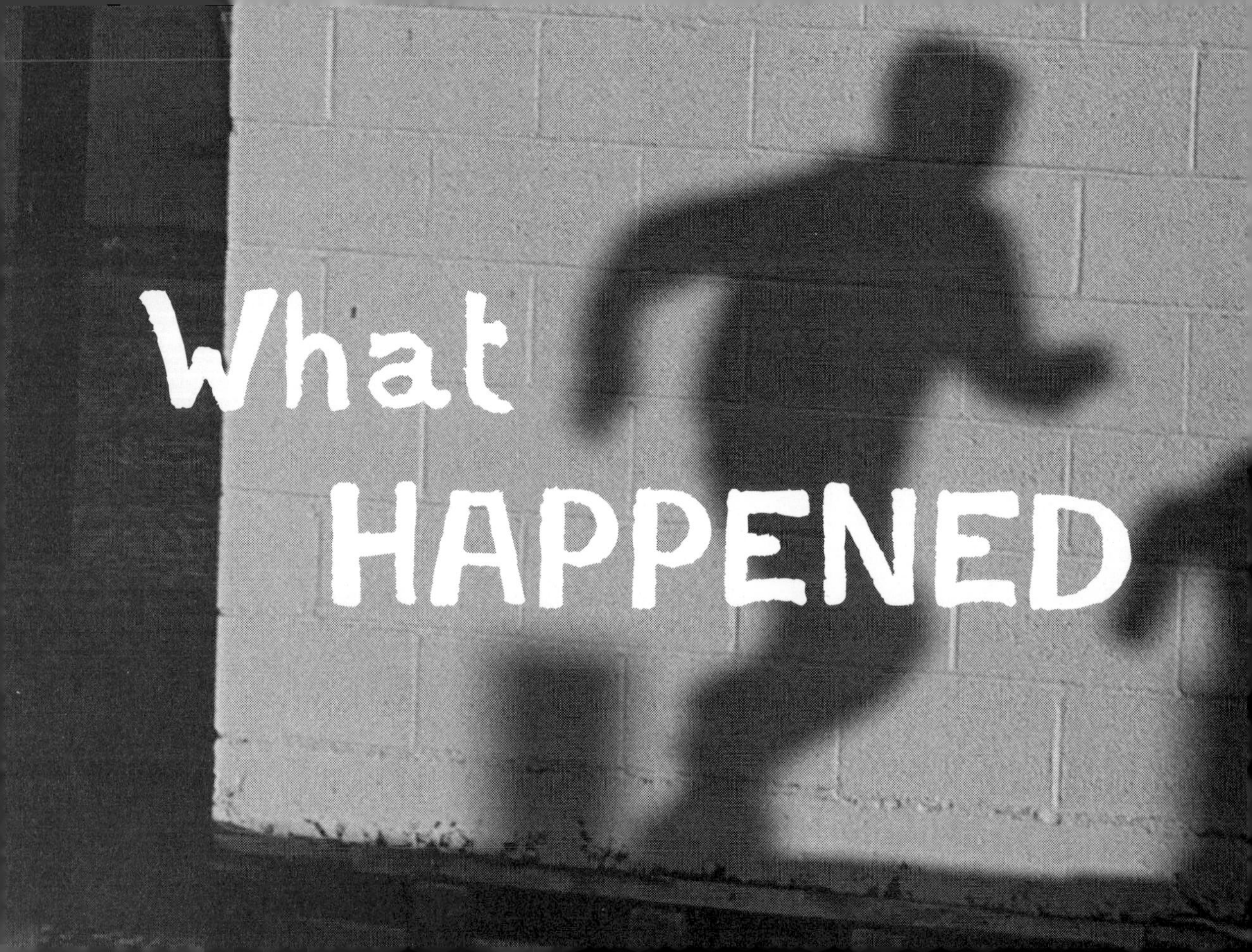
What
HAPPENED

to it?

PART THREE

'I was quaking in my little wee jandals.'

Sonja Yelich

25
Who KILLED bullrush?

Sonja Yelich was just a tiny little kid, hauled into Mrs Woods' office. Mrs Woods was the deputy principal. 'She gave me what for. I was quaking in my little wee jandals. She said this is absolutely … somebody could be killed.'

You were emphatically not permitted to play bullrush at Gladstone Primary, in the early 1970s. Little Sonja's bigger brother — 'he was a giant of a kid' — had started a game anyway. He thought it would be good. 'And you just could not play that at our school.

'I didn't even know what actually happened in the game because I never saw it occur. And I was mortified. I just remember being so humiliated. We were already a stand-out bad family, but I remember being so humiliated, being called into the horrid Mrs Woods' office, to know that my brother was doing such a thing.'

Another boy, Todd Marinovich, wanted to play it too, a few years later. He thought he would start the game up again. He was in a big lot of trouble.

'Somebody could be killed; a broken neck. They were always talking about somebody could have a broken neck. It was the neck thing. When you're a kid, you know that if an adult's talking about a broken neck, you're not going to play it, whether that makes any sense to you or not. A broken neck and somebody could get killed were synonymous with bullrush.'

It wasn't the only time she was called to the office. There was a ditch at the end of the school grounds and her brother was building a human trap. 'He was in big trouble for that too. He had sticks and twigs and they were going to get kids to walk across and fall in there.'

As seen on TV? 'I don't think so. That was the seventies. I don't think they were doing that on *The Brady Bunch* or *The Waltons* or *Happy Days*.'

At her own kids' primary school in Devonport, some of the trees had a white line. Don't climb above the white line. 'If it had an X on it, that meant you could climb it. But actually it was pretty cool they were allowed to climb the trees.'

They weren't allowed at Gladstone. And they had a lot of trees.

Her favourite playtime game — and everybody's favourite — was Cowboys and Indians.

It was just a game of chase and capture. Some of you were Indians, some were Cowboys and off you went. Nobody got hurt. 'We liked to play it because then a boy could catch you and I quite liked that.'

He could have caught her in bullrush too. 'Oh no, you'd get hurt! You could get a broken neck! I didn't ever want to play a game where I was going to be hurt. I was tall and skinny and my bones could easily snap. No monkey business like that for me. But certainly my brother, he liked all those body-crunching games.' They liked to watch *On the Mat*. You could get good moves from that — like King Curtis — take that to school with you and see what you could get away with.

This is the truth about the way things get banned in schools: it has a lot to do with what the deputy principal thinks; it has not very much to do with bureaucrats.

Where did bullrush go? A decent number of schools today permit a supervised tag version of the game — no tackling, a light tap on the shoulders, arms or upper back. A few have happily declared to the media in recent years that they permit bullrush, albeit some with mouthguards and other sorts of protection.

Hereworth School in Havelock North allows it, so do Seven Oaks School in Christchurch, and Royal Road in Massey, Auckland. You can play it at Woodleigh School, New Plymouth, at Mt Biggs School near Feilding. You can play it without any rules at all at Swanson School in West Auckland, as we'll see shortly.

Some schools just say no. The aim of the behaviour management programme at Paihia School, stated on their website, is 'to have an atmosphere throughout the school in which children feel cared for, secure and happy, and have the maximum opportunity to learn'. It's a long list, and under 'ensuring the safety of self and others' is this rule: No rough play, fighting, play-fighting or bullrush.

In the UK in 2013, more than a quarter of 653 school staff surveyed by the Association of Teachers and Lecturers said British Bulldog had been banned from their school. One in ten said they'd also banned leapfrog.

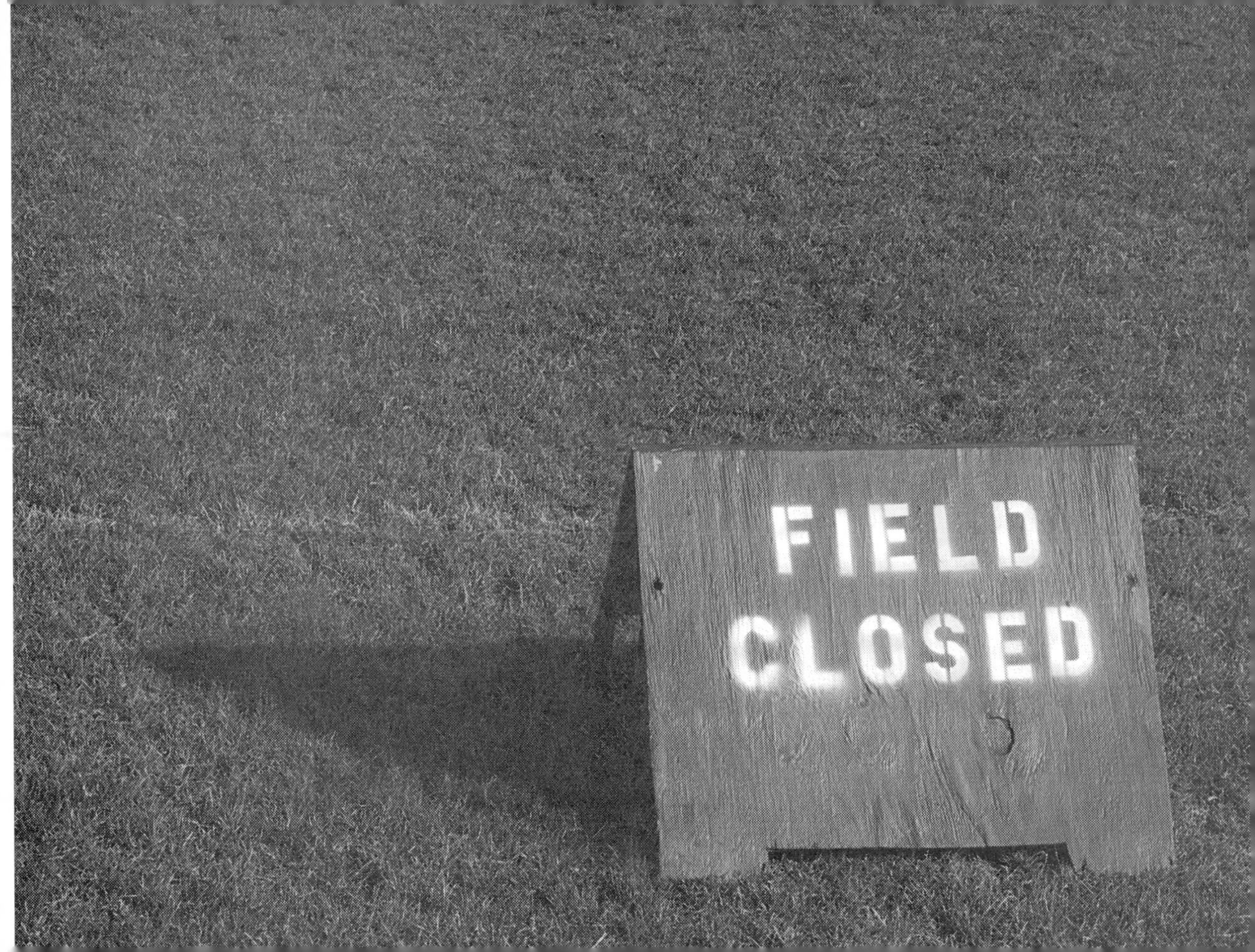
FIELD
CLOSED

Nearly two thirds of them said they felt schools were becoming increasingly risk-averse. Why? Fewer staff to supervise activities, not enough funding, concerns over pupil safety, they said. One said bulldog was banned 'because of the number of broken bones it generates'.

There was one British principal who banned tag because big kids tend to get too great a share of the spoils. Also, nominating one child as a victim creates a potential self-esteem issue.

In Queensland, a teacher offers a modernised, safer version of the game — 'Bulldog if implemented safely can develop and refine children's skills under increasing pressure.' He says it only takes a simple rule change: tackling is omitted and capturing an opponent is identified through the use of 'flag belts'.

It makes the singing Japanese version sound positively edgy and dangerous.

When people lament that something has the look of PC gone mad, the blame can often fall on some kind of nazi — a health nazi, a feminazi — but mostly it will fall on 'them'. Who won't let you do this? 'They' won't let you. Who came up with this ridiculous rule? 'They' did. Them, they, or some faceless bureaucrat.

New Zealand schools enjoy large latitude. If they choose to be constrained, they'll be constrained. If they choose to be loose, they'll be loose. If Mrs Woods thinks you'll get a broken neck, you will not play bullrush at your school.

You will search in vain for a bureaucrat who will tell you that a school is forbidden from playing bullrush.

'Did you do it,' I ask the Ministry of Education, 'did you ban bullrush?'

'No,' they said.

'Is there any rule that says bullrush cannot be played?'

'No,' they said.

'Well, is there a more general rule about what can be played in the playgrounds? Is there any edict at all about what can or cannot be played in the grounds?'

'No,' they said.

Yes, schools are required to provide a safe environment, but how they do it is over to them.

How about WorkSafe, the organisation formerly known as OSH? Do they have a rule about it? Have they ever prosecuted a school for playing it? Do they have any requirements about this?

'Not us,' they said, 'maybe you should talk to the Ministry of Education.'

Well, what about the fog of anxiety that drifted across the land as, for example, a couple were prosecuted for the death in 1994 of a visiting beekeeper on their King Country farm land after a bridge collapsed under him, a bridge built by the army, which as far as they knew was quite safe?

What if, in the early 1990s, that fog of anxiety rolled in over the new school boards of trustees created by the Tomorrow's Schools programmes? And what if those new boards fretted about the new health and safety legislation?

It was quite a scary-looking new law, what with its personal liability and all. The intention was to see that you didn't backslide on your obligations to keep people safe in your workplace. But what if it had the effect of taking too much of the play out of our playgrounds?

A trustee on a school board might look at this new law and worry a little, especially the lawyer kind. They might draw the board's attention to this scary legislation. They might draw the board's attention in particular to this bit about personal liability as a trustee. They might recommend an abundance of caution.

They more than likely wouldn't get prosecuted just because a kid got hurt in the playground. But what if? they might think to themselves, what if a bullrush game might lead all the way to your being personally liable for it? Maybe there's a quieter game the kids could be playing.

So did fretful school boards kill bullrush? It's one possibility. You can talk to retired principals but you'll struggle to find even one who can specifically remember banning it. They suggest it would most likely have happened like this: someone's child got hurt, a shirt got ripped, their parent complained to the school. It happened again, the parent complained with a little more energy. If it looked as though it might not be readily resolved, a teacher or a principal might look at everything else on their plate and say: it's not worth dying in a ditch over this. So they might say: look, let's just ban the game, it's the easiest way to deal with it. The squeaky wheel stops the bullrush.

Once, if their child was injured at school, parents tended to say it was just one of those things. If the kid got in trouble, they tended to side with the school, unless they were little Tommy Scott's mother. Not so much these days. Whatever the school does, every trip, sport, they must have the parents' consent. They must consult with the parents. The parent in this new power balance is a different quantity, and not necessarily a placid one.

This sits in a larger picture. Parents fret about their children. We can walk a strutting talk about individual freedom when we're finding fault with other people but in our own lives, in our own decision-making, like a lawyer on a school board, we can be cautious to a fault. We can be relaxed as a summer's day right up until the moment there's an accident, and then the helicopter parent emerges and reaches for the lawyer.

We don't let our own kids roam. In 2013, researchers at the University of Virginia interviewed 100 parents. Nearly all of them remembered childhoods of nearly unlimited freedom, when they could roam at will, but when it comes to their own children, they can't imagine giving their children that same freedom. They worry about the harm they might come to, they worry about abduction.

We can be relaxed as a summer's day right up until the moment there's an accident.

Yet crime figures show the risk is remote. In the USA in 1999, only 115 children nationwide were kidnapped by a stranger. That same year, 2931 children under fifteen died as passengers in car accidents.

Elsewhere in the world, parents may sue. One popular theory sees the story begin in Chicago in the early 1970s with a playground accident. A child dropped through a gap at the top of a very tall slide, onto the concrete below, and hurt her head dreadfully. Successful legal action followed, ambulance-chasing lawyers followed that legal action with much more, right across the nation, suits against any public authority where they found a playground and a hurt child. Regulations followed; antiseptic plastic playgrounds followed that.

Parents fret, parents sue, everyone gets defensive and cautious. But if a parent really wanted to perturb a school principal, there's no denying there are some frightening newspaper clippings they can show them.

Eight-year-old Freya James of London was in the worst place in the school playground at the worst possible time. While she was playing some other game, she was hit by a boy playing British Bulldog and got knocked onto a playground ornament made from a recycled railway sleeper. She died in hospital of internal bleeding two hours later.

In Nebraska, a ten-year-old boy died from brain injuries he sustained colliding with a metal pole while playing tag.

A school dinner lady in Dorset was left partially paralysed after a thirteen-year-old boy playing tag ran into her in 2004. Significantly, her claim for damage was rejected by three Court of Appeal judges, who ruled the boy had not broken any school rules by playing the game.

What's really at issue here is risk — how much we take and how we balance it.

What happens, a lot, is this: rather than have to make the risk assessment, people, businesses, school boards often elect to take the easy way out. They say no, we can't, honestly, our hands are tied. Health and safety rules say we're not allowed. This is often nonsense. They just don't want to have to think about it. They don't want to have to do the risk assessment.

The BBC quotes a head teacher, venting about health and safety rules: 'It's ridiculous. If it's slightly wet, we don't let them go on the grass in case they fall and we get sued.' Schools are worrying about legal action and prosecution that almost never happens, the Health and Safety Executive says. They're not concerned with children playing games. If they sensibly manage the risks involved in children's play, they won't be at risk of prosecution.

Also: 'There has never been a nationwide ban on British Bulldog,' says a spokesman for the Department for Children, Schools and Families.

The Health and Safety Executive in the UK runs a 'myth of the month' slot on its website. They banned egg boxes from school craftwork to avoid spreading salmonella. Not us. Hard hats for trapeze artists. No.

Whatever reason people have come up with, being against the law is not the right one.

When are you really in danger? What's your largest risk? For almost anything that doesn't involve methamphetamine and semi-automatic weapons, it's getting into a car. If we were properly careful about it we'd still be driving at 10 kph with a person walking ahead of the car, waving a flag. If we were really, really careful, we would never get out of bed in the morning.

Who killed bullrush, then?

Schools have their fingerprints on the gun, yes. But you might more accurately say we did it to ourselves. A teacher might have fired the gun, but only because it was the easiest thing to do, after fretful parents put that gun in their hand.

You really can't argue that — even wildly indirectly — they did it, that some faceless bureaucrat is at fault here.

What we can see, though, is a culture of caution in many schools today, and we can see a generation of kids being driven to and from those schools wrapped up in nice snug cotton wool.

How we seem to be dealing with this is not encouraging. We tend to swing wildly between two points of view moved by sentiment more than reason. At a moment of calamity, our mood is agitated: something has gone wrong; somebody must be to blame.

But on those days when nothing is going wrong, a different parent comes out to play: Why on earth are these nanny state busybodies being so ridiculously cautious?

We can only be thankful that today's media is so dependably measured and proportionate about these things, loath to judge prematurely, and scrupulous about getting all the facts and the full context, that things never get out of hand.

26
Running with scissors

The principal of Swanson Primary School, Bruce McLachlan — Mr Mac to the kids — is no zealot. He's lived long enough to know what you should worry about, and he's sure he's right about this: sometimes the best thing an adult can do for children is get out of the way.

At Swanson School, there are no rules about play. At Swanson School if you want to, you can play bullrush. At Swanson School, you could run with scissors if you wanted to, but no-one does.

When Mr Mac was a kid, the playgrounds were an acre of danger. You pitched as high as you could go in swings, with chains that you caught your fingers in and when you came off a roundabout or a swing you learned to not do that again.

Nobody was too concerned about the skin and arms and skinned knees.

Today's playground equipment is different. No sharp edges, elaborate. He calls them plastic fantastics. They look really interesting, if you're an adult: a valuable, educational tool for kids to play with. 'But in fact the kids find them boring.'

They haven't had a plastic fantastic in their playground for nearly three years. 'And this playground is one of the most settled, warm, inviting and yet active playgrounds in most schools that you will see. The kids aren't playing on structures designed by adults. They're actually playing in the world, which is what kids have done for hundreds of thousands of years.'

It began with a university study looking for ways to tackle obesity and bullying. How they did it was up to them. Mr Mac decided to take away all the rules about play. 'We weren't allowing them to have the kinds of experiences that I had in the sixties when I was growing up.'

The 1960s. Those reckless, feckless days, when parents let us roam, untracked, unmonitored, untroubled. How did we come through it alive?

When you're on your own, he says, you don't automatically do bad things. 'Nor do you do dangerous things. Adults today worry about kids. They worry that if you leave them alone to their own devices, they will do something bad, or wrong, and they'll hurt themselves and they'll hurt others. In fact, that isn't what happens.'

People don't go out into the world intending to hurt themselves. They naturally protect themselves, and so do children. 'Even though they're not adults, they do it. It's a natural human thing.'

The more he looked at it, the more he was sure: adults had become far too involved in children's play. 'What happens whenever we're with kids? We want to protect and look after them and care for them. It's our instinct. It's completely understandable, it's admirable. But we're getting in the way.'

The bell goes. Kids spill into the playground. You won't see these scenes in most schools, he says. People when they see this for the first time say, 'Oh my God, kids are going to get hurt.' He points across the playground. 'A couple of girls there wearing helmets. Most of our kids don't wear helmets.

But if their kids were doing tricks that involved them possibly hurting themselves, he says, 'then until they learned the trick they would wear a helmet.' They had a boy who brought in some Oscar Pistorius-type stilts. Did the most amazing things around the school, 'but because he knew that he was possibly going to end up on his head, he wore his helmet'.

What about the child who actually hurts themselves and can seriously hurt themselves — what about a head injury? You worry about the highly likely things that can happen to everybody, he says, not the one time in 10,000. There have been in the four years they've been doing this literally tens of thousands of movements involving kids on scooters, on bikes, skateboards and not a single serious injury. Not one. 'And even if a kid got seriously injured, I would be working very hard to not change the policy.'

Adults don't only design the structures, they also design the rules. When they see kids wandering around doing 'nothing' they think those kids need to be organised into a game; they'll bustle the kids into a formal game, of soccer or netball or rugby, which is great for people who love sports, but children by and large tend to just want to have fun.

Adults don't have any input into play other than a negative one. Play is ideally a blank canvas rather than one that has been three quarters filled in. 'The kinds of sports we get our kids involved in are often for the entertainment of the adults on the sideline. Give kids an opportunity to play a game of cricket or to climb a tree, some kids will choose the game of cricket, absolutely. And we should be always giving those kids those opportunities. But we should also be giving them the opportunity to climb a tree.'

The kids are still playing. All of them are barefooted. Many of them are even doubling up on the scooters or bike or trike, seeing how they can load the second passenger on.

'You'll see little kids mixed up with big kids. A lot of schools separate little kids and big kids in the playground because of the assumption that adults have about children that they will hurt themselves or they will hurt others.' But this is what actually happens when a child is hooning towards another child and one of them's got a scooter: it's like driving through a pedestrian mall. 'The child on the scooter is going to learn to look out for the kids who aren't, and the kids who aren't on the scooter are going to look out for the kid who's on the scooter.'

That's a lesson he wants kids to learn. Take away the opportunities for them to experience those things, how do they learn it?

We watch some of the kids on these scooters and the tricks they do. Impressive skills. They're all moving; there are so many smiling faces. It's a very, very happy place.

Kids these days, we hear, will park themselves in front of a screen and stay there. Many schools ban devices. Swanson doesn't. Most of their kids would probably have an iPod or a phone with them. But they don't choose to use it. They choose to be active.

When adults become involved in the play experience the kids aren't getting hurt. This is not a good thing. 'Being hurt is actually quite an important part of growing up. Adults worry that children will go out and hurt themselves and hurt others. Their instinct is to wrap

them up in cotton wool. Most kids — we're not talking about the potential criminals — most kids do the right thing.'

It's the same when they run the risk of hurting themselves. 'If a kid wants to try a new trick and they see the others doing it, and they want to be able to do it, nine times out of ten they'll recognise that they're going to get hurt.' Sometimes they will make a choice to get hurt or to risk getting hurt, just as we adults do. We manage risk all the time. In the playground at Swanson School each playtime, the kids learn how to do it.

What did the parents think about this revolution? 'Well, actually I didn't ask them. I say jokingly that I prefer to ask for forgiveness than for permission — but there's a certain truth to that. We actually just started turning a blind eye to everything the kids were doing in the playground that didn't matter.'

It was teachers, rather than parents, who needed the most persuasion. What if the kids got hurt? He told them he would take that blame.

He told them: 'If you don't want to watch a kid climbing a tree, don't look.' Kids know that when there are no adults there to look, they have to take charge.

They do what is right for them, what is natural for them. 'And what is natural for them is to be active, to climb, to swing, to communicate with others, to cooperate, to push people around and learn to be pushed around and to move the amount of pushing around that I'm prepared to take before I lash out, to lash out and see what happens.'

When he first came to Swanson School, teachers on duty at playtime were busy. They carried a bag with sticking plasters and bandages, they told kids to stop playing with that, to put that down. There was a detention room and rigmarole. Not any more.

They had a TV crew here filming the kids. One came out of the tree, bleeding. 'You've cut your arm,' the reporter said. The kid looked down, inspected it, shrugged, said, 'Oh yeah.'

'It was a brilliant camera moment,' Mr Mac remembers. 'Blood doesn't mean the same thing as it used to.'

One of the two duty teachers strolls past our window, holding her coffee cup. There is no bullying. There is no conflict. There are no serious injuries in the

'Being hurt is actually quite an important part of growing up.'

Bruce McLachlan

playground. When it's necessary, big boys or mates step in and pull people apart. If little kids get a grazed knee, other kids come and help them. 'What is happening outside of the view of adults,' he says, 'is not *Lord of the Flies*, but rather what we would like the world to be. It's adults who are nasty, selfish, jealous, violent creatures, not kids.'

What about the safety laws? OSH/WorkSafe has become a scary monster for many, many people since its inception, he says; it doesn't need to be. Safety laws require him to identify hazards or potential hazards. But there's hardly a thing on the surface of the earth that couldn't be defined as a hazard, if you have a strong enough aversion to risk.

He points to a deadly office occasional table beside his desk. He could trip over that. He could! He might hurt himself to the extent that he might break his neck and die. He could! 'Do we define that table as a hazard? We don't.' Where a more risk-averse school might say, 'I'm going to get rid of that drain, I'm going to stop the kids playing in that spiky tree. I'm going to stop the kids from riding bikes', he is more likely to be recording the fact that a garden hose or a pipe or a tree or an occasional table could be a hazard and leaving it at that.

There are two questions all the reporters ask Mr Mac. Firstly: How come you're ignoring the rule that you're not allowed to play bullrush? And secondly: Is that in fact a rule? 'And of course it wasn't. It was never a rule. There are all sorts of rules that we assume are rules in society that aren't rules.'

At the outset he held a staff meeting. Write down what our rules are in the playground, he asked them. 'And you had people busy writing away down there, pages and pages.' In fact, they didn't have any. No such thing existed.

He's had a total of two negative conversations with parents about the policy in four years. 'A member of the parent community came in one day. My secretary said, "You know so-and-so's son who broke his arm in the playground the other day? He wants to talk to you." I had all of these apologies in mind, and he came in and he said, "My boy got hurt in the playground the other day. I don't want you to change anything." And he ended up being on the Board of Trustees.'

Not everyone's a believer. His daughter teaches in a school in Christchurch. TV's *60 Minutes* programme told the Swanson School story and school staff rooms were talking about it the next day. Everybody in the staff room at her school said how neat it was but how impractical it was to make any changes to what they were doing. You'll get a lot of that, he says. That is being risk-averse.

'You see how happy the kids are, how our academic statistics are as good as other schools', our stand-down and suspension rate is heaps better, I can't remember the last time an ambulance was called to the school — all of those sorts of things — and yet we're not the norm. It doesn't feel more normal to people who come in here but to us it feels normal.'

The Education Review Office treads a little gingerly. 'Last time they were here I think they struggled to criticise too much because they can see the benefits of it. Being risk-averse, they were still worried, but it wasn't something that we were required to change.'

The Ministry of Education has never said anything to him about it. They've talked about it around the smoko table, he's been told, but they haven't looked at it in any formal policy sense.

Kids don't change, only their circumstances do. He thinks maybe the generations before this one were a bit more physically skilled, but look at their hand–eye coordination these days. 'There's a lot of jet pilots around who grew up on game consoles. Kids change as the world changes but they don't become any less moral.'

He'd like to see bullrush flourish again, he would. 'We have the most amazing tradition in rugby that I think we need to be proud of. For Josh Kronfeld to say that for him bullrush was part of the reason why he became such a good All Black, I think that's very important.'

But he wonders if it might be gone. There's very little bullrush played at Swanson School. Not because it is banned but because it dropped from view and out of consciousness.

'I think we've lost bullrush to the annals of time because a lot of young adults didn't have the opportunity to play it. If kids have never seen it, how will it occur to them to play it?'

But he also doesn't want to tell them how they should play. They need to be given the blank canvas. Not the picture to colour in.

'If you don't want to watch a kid climbing a tree, don't look. '

Bruce McLachlan

27
Boys will be 120 kg

Can you play bullrush at Wellington College? No. Theoretically, it's banned these days, says the principal, Roger Moses.

'There's been a lot of talk about boys not being allowed to be boys. Well, in a boys' school you don't get away with that and nor would I want to. Now there are some who would oppose it on philosophical grounds — and I say to that, bunkum. You know — what a terrible thing it is to be teaching aggression, all the rest of it. No. It's boys being boys.

'We're not philosophically opposed to bullrush at all. I think they can be a lot of fun. The danger, I guess is this: boys are getting bigger. I was in the Auckland Grammar first fifteen as a loose forward at ten and a half stone. I wouldn't get

a look-in these days. I can think of when Neemia Tialata was in our front row here and he was actually smaller when he played for the All Blacks than when he played for us. So I wonder to what extent the sheer size of boys and the hardness of hits and all that sort of stuff has become a problem.'

Lunch break at Wellington College you'll see games going the whole time — touch games, semi tackle games. Sometimes it becomes tackle stuff as well — and they'll say no tackling, boys, because you can end up after lunchtime with a room full of damaged goods.

They're not going to stop kids getting out there and having games. 'That wouldn't be very popular here. But what we have to be a little bit careful of is if one of these games became downright dangerous, and if a little fella is trying to tackle a huge bloke who may be 120 kg, there can be some real carnage in the process.

'Look, I've got no opposition to boys getting outside throwing themselves around. I've been running a boys' school for twenty years now. Boys love a physical game at lunchtime. And I don't mean they're going to try and knock each other's block off all the time, but they enjoy a physical game. It's part of what they do. It's a blowout. But sometimes we just have to step in and say hey boys, we've gotta cut that one back a bit. I think that in a big boys' school like ours, the potential for carnage is so much greater than it used to be.

'I can think back two or three years ago a game of bullrush where one of our kids, Nelson Asofa-Solomona — he came regarded as one of the hottest properties in secondary school rugby, he's now playing for Melbourne Storm — Nelson at school was about six foot six, a hundred and twenty kg and of course when he joined in to play it was just carnage. I'm still in regular touch with the kid — he's a wonderful boy. But he's massive! He's absolutely huge. These guys are miles, miles bigger than Colin Meads ever was.'

There are injuries all the time, just as there are in a rugby match. Sometimes there have been broken arms, there have occasionally been broken legs, dislocated this and that. You know it's going to happen. But no lasting harm. No-one in a wheelchair.

'I think even some of our footy coaches are concerned when good kids go and injure themselves. That may be an issue — that increasingly with the professionalism we're seeing in sport even at secondary level, boys are looking after themselves much more carefully than they did before. There are professional careers at risk here.

'If you were to go back twenty years and just see the difference in the power some of these kids can put into it. At the point of contact there is potentially much more damage being done and this may well have been something that has quietly evolved with the kind of pick-up games like bullrush and it probably led to schools saying hey guys, good fun but too dangerous.'

Could Tomorrow's Schools and health and safety law changes have chilled the playgrounds? Could it be what killed bullrush? 'I wouldn't say it was a direct

thing with bullrush but there's probably an element of truth in it. I don't want to be cynical about that — I think if you're taking kids away on overnight hikes or anything like that, you do have to be careful. But certainly there is considerably more red tape that we have to work through now than would've been the case some years ago.'

They have a forty-hour runathon for World Vision. It raises huge amounts of money — $50,000 to $70,000. 'One of the things they do is this big medicine ball, where two boys charge at each other and they bounce off each other and of course that causes a great deal of mirth. But we did it last year and one little fella got knocked out in the process. And so I guess what we're seeing is that while human nature doesn't change, I guess there is a little more sensitivity now around prevention of injury.

'I think that these kind of games, they tend to resurface in all shapes and forms,' he says. Wellington College has a brand-new artificial turf, where they can play both rugby and football and all kinds of other permutations and combinations of games 'which involve the expending of great bucketloads of testosterone'.

He recalls one sport that has disappeared off the face of the earth. 'We have old boys coming back asking: Do you still have fives?' It was a huge sport at Auckland Grammar, it was huge at Wellington College. There are still five courts remaining. Three on each side and you played with a tennis ball.

'It was a massive sport. Huge sport. I think it must have been gone at the end of the fifties. These schoolyard sports do come and go. We've still got cups here that were presented for fives. You talk to any of these guys who are now in their seventies and eighties. And they will talk about fives. That's where the fives courts used to be. So I guess things come and go.'

Barry Brickell built several kilometres of railway in the Coromandel with his bare hands. If you farewell him with 'Take care', he will reply: 'No. Take risks, carefully.'

We worry that children born since the advent of television can't organise their own entertainment. We worry that they're addicted to spectator amusements and Grand Theft Auto. We fill their days with classes and play dates and play material and we helicopter them.

We worry that they're not learning how to take risks, and we keep them insulated from risk all day long.

Except: maybe our kids are finding a different set of risks. They may not be taking the ones we took, but God knows they take one every time they start typing on Facebook, on Snapchat, on YouTube, on sites you've never heard of. We scared ourselves to death over nuclear war; they can get the same sinking feeling about climate change.

If we got smart about this, we'd step back a bit and let them take a few more risks. We could also do something about our carbon emissions.

Will we see

it again?

PART FOUR

Bullrush is a game for friends. Play it as much as you damn well like.

28
Going back

The finest game of bullrush you will ever see is three and a half minutes long and you will find it on YouTube. Excitement, good-natured ribbing, and the slightest sensation of terror; a squad of Lions and All Blacks on the London Metropolitan Police Rugby ground.

It begins with Tana Umaga alone in the middle, entirely untroubled, amused. Along the try line are forty-odd test rugby players, grinning, poised. 'Bring it,' says Tana, casually beckoning.

Here they come, all 3200–4000 kg of them. Tana sidesteps a little, scanning for his best prospect. Tana's all over him. McCaw looks back over his shoulder, smirking as he slows down to the try line.

They run again, another couple come down. The middle begins to fill.

Doug Howlett is going fast and hard, ducking, weaving. Richie, loafing, looks across to follow the spectacle. To his complete surprise he's tackled from behind and down he goes, planted. Never saw it coming.

Tana's looking a bit puffed as they line up for another go, but he already has half a dozen men alongside him and they all look hungry and keen.

Richie is doing some *hard work*. One guy after another hits the ground; red, black, doesn't matter. You bastards are coming down.

Now some huge forwards are tipping over, two or three backs, maybe four or five of them all hanging off you and down you come.

But look at Joe Rokococo! He's full of running, no trouble. Nobody can get a hand on him.

Slowly, steadily, more of them fill the middle. For a while, it's red and black, tackling madly, and then almost everyone's been brought down.

Except for Joe Rokococo and Brian O'Driscoll, alone now on the try line, looking down the field, to a solid wall of test rugby players. How in God's name do you get past that?

This is what you remember about bullrush. The sheer ridiculous impossibility of it as you get near the end. And yet sometimes someone found a way through. Will Joe? Will Brian? They come across the line warily. They start to pick up speed. They move faster and faster towards the wall of men and … the video ends.

They were filming it for an adidas advert. James Sikora's job was Senior Manager, Global Sports Marketing. He had a ball that day, he remembers. Everyone did. No-one had any playing commitments, so they'd all been on the turps the night before. The bus was just full of really, really hung-over dudes at seven o'clock that morning.

At the pre-shoot briefing, the instruction was emphatic: 'No injuries; we can't afford any of that.' But within thirty minutes of togging up, everyone was into it. Like, seriously. Never mind 'No hits, no injuries, we can't afford any of that': twenty minutes in, they were just going full-on contact. You can't legislate for some things.

That's the appeal of the game, isn't it? You want to rise to the challenge. You want to bring the guy down. 'I think it tells you about the guys who play the game,' James says. 'It was schoolboys, it really was. Everyone who was watching it wanted to get out and have a go as well.'

Seven o'clock in the morning to five-thirty p.m. They played *all day*. They were highly skilled, the people who'd choreographed it. 'But really, choreography went out the window as soon as it started. You're playing the game. You're nailing people.

'One of the things I loved was McCaw missing a hit on Byron Kelleher and Richie got genuinely pissed about that. Absolutely smoking. If you look at the video you'll see Richie gets an arm out and Wazza's just laughing and cackling and McCaw is really, really not happy. And then he just smashes him from behind.'

The idea was to illustrate how, when it comes down to it, rugby players are the same wherever they're from. 'And that's how it wound up, because you started getting Lions guys on the one side and All Blacks on the same side and Lions and All Blacks guys on the other side. It worked out. It wasn't All Blacks and Lions — it was a bunch of guys wearing black and red shirts, and having a bit of craic and lovin' it. Having the time of their lives, hung-over as hell, but still loving it.'

The ad leaves you wondering what happened. *How could they do that?* They didn't want to imply an outcome for the Lions series. The following year Brian O'Driscoll would be the first man off the pitch on a stretcher, double spear-tackled off the ball within one minute of the first test match, out for the series. One day you're a rooster, the next you're playing rugby.

We're grown-ups. If we want to play bullrush again, there really isn't a thing in the world to stop us.

Sam Ward has a gym in Albany. You get a lot of banter in a gym. They were swapping cheek: who's tougher, rugby guys or league ones? 'We said we'd settle it with a game of bullrush. We put it on Facebook and a few people got excited.

That got me excited and I thought we'd do it in the stadium instead of just a park and it snowballed from there.'

The TIKA Bullrush Pro-Am was held on a specially painted pitch at North Harbour Stadium on a Saturday in November in 2013. Hundreds came. So did some biblical weather, right on kick-off time. It dampened numbers a little bit but not spirits.

They got the players into the changing sheds, divvied them into sections: kids, teenagers, under-eighty-five section, open weight. The man in the middle would be a volunteer who got a free life through to the next round. Or something like that.

People were fizzing. Absolutely fizzing. 'Yeah, everyone loved it, even the spectators loved it. It was a good spectacle.'

Richard 'Rigger' James got a prize for running the length of the field without being tackled. Louise Anderton, the only woman taking part, made it almost to the final. The winner of the open men's category was Sefa Tuiasau, 'an absolute legend'.

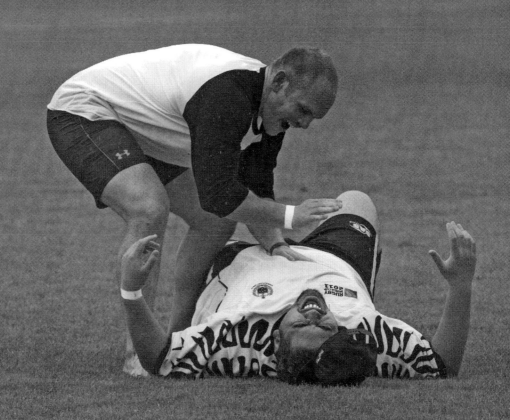

He'll do it again at some point, Sam, if life stops getting in the way. He's relocated the business, he's married, there's always something. But the template's there and they've spoken to a few people. It's a lot of work but they'd love to run it again.

It's not what you play, in the end, it's how you play it. Consider, for example, the Philippines. They love their karaoke singing there. But only until some clown gets up and sings 'My Way' the wrong way. Regrets, they have a few. At least a half dozen times it has ended in violent homicide: the 'My Way' killing phenomenon, they call it.

Karaoke rage is not peculiar to the Philippines. People have been shot, stabbed, taken apart with a meat cleaver, just for getting their singing wrong. Endless renditions of John Denver's 'Take Me Home, Country Roads' can earn you a beating. A karaoke singer in Seattle was punched and punched and punched again by a woman who absolutely emphatically did not care to hear him sing the Coldplay song 'Yellow'.

You never saw that kind of thing in bullrush. Bullrush is a game for friends.

Play it as much as you damn well like.

Bullrush was the game we made our own, like rugby. Perhaps it was just a happy accident of propitious circumstances: soft grounds, a kind climate. We charged up and down the paddocks growing as big and strong as the livestock.

Perhaps we should have been inside longer, reading more, and perhaps it was lucky we weren't. John Mulgan's *Report on Experience* describes New Zealanders in the Second World War.

'I found in wartime that there was a considerable virtue in men who had played games like professionals to win, and not, like public school boys and amateurs, for exercise.'

Mulgan remembered this about the country: rugby was the best of all our pleasures. It was religion and desire and fulfilment all in one. A lot of thinkers might feel that an exaggerated attention to games gives you the wrong sense of values. Or maybe: not so much wrong as primitive. You might hope for other, higher, better values in a civilised age, but at a time of monstrous war, this was the kind of person you wanted to be fighting with.

The instruction was emphatic: 'No injuries.' But within thirty minutes everyone was into it.

The New Zealanders were men who, in war, found themselves able to get down to the moral plane of the German soldier, even think a ruse or two ahead. 'In the game of total war Englishmen spent some time and casualties in finding war ungentlemanly before they tossed the rules overboard.'

He didn't think those things affected the natural kindliness of the New Zealanders, nor the kind of ethics they expected from people in private life. It was only that they looked on war as a game. A deadly game. A game, to New Zealanders, was something you played to win, against the other side and the referee if necessary.

Maybe bullrush is lost to the annals of time, just a golden memory to take with us. Perhaps for those of us who grew up in those simpler post-war boom years, it was just our special thing.

Good luck to the kids. It would be just great if they could have as much fun as we did. I hope they get the chance.

Kids will go on tagging and chasing for as long as they can run. They will. They'll find new ways of playing on screens, they'll be digital, they'll have vastly different childhoods from us, and they'll eventually locate risk somewhere no matter how ridiculously difficult we make it for them. Maybe one day an unimaginably long time from now they'll find a way to play on Mars.

Man, bullrush would be *awesome* there.

Standing in the middle

Michèle A'Court was Comedienne of the Decade at the 2010 NZ Comedy Awards. She is a prolific columnist and commentator, and the author of *Stuff I Forgot To Tell My Daughter*.

Jacinda Ardern is a Labour List MP based in Auckland Central and is party spokesperson on Justice and Arts, Culture and Heritage.

Len Brown is Mayor of Auckland.

Frank Bunce, All Black, played four tests for Samoa and 55 for New Zealand.

Wallace Chapman is the host of *Sunday Morning* on Radio New Zealand, co-host of cult 'pub politics' TV show *Back Benches*, and author of *Don't Just Do Something, Sit There: A Manifesto for Living the Slow Life*.

Rodney Hide was a member of parliament and ACT party leader.

Robert Kelly is a Wellington-based writer, house painter, recent ex-student and occasionally employed.

Josh Kronfeld played 54 tests for the All Blacks including appearances at the 1995 and 1999 Rugby World Cups.

Michelle Langstone has starred in films and television series ranging from *Power Rangers* to *The Almighty Johnsons* and *Go Girls*.

Brendhan Lovegrove is a comedian and public speaker and a regular at The Classic comedy bar in Auckland.

Greg McGee is a writer and playwright celebrated for his first play *Foreskin's Lament* and a host of TV credits including *Erebus: The Aftermath*, and *Fallout*. He co-wrote movie scripts for *Crooked Earth*, *Via Satellite* and *Old Scores*. He has also written acclaimed crime novels as Alix Bosco.

Robyn Malcolm is a vastly accomplished actress, best known for her role as Cheryl West in *Outrageous Fortune*.

Keith Douglas 'Midge' Marsden is an R&B guitarist, harmonica player, and singer, with a musical career spanning four decades.

Scotty Morrison is a current affairs presenter for *Te Karere* and *Marae Investigates*. He has been an Adjunct Professor at Auckland's Unitec Institute of Technology and is the author of *The Raupo Phrasebook of Modern Maori*.

Stacey Morrison has hosted TV shows *What Now*, *Mai Time*, *It's In The Bag* and *Re-Think*. In radio she has been a host on Mai FM, Flava and Classic Hits FM. Stacey and Scotty Morrison married in 2006.

Te Radar (born Andrew J. Lumsden) is a comedian, compere and eponymous hero of such TV shows as *Off the Radar*, *Homegrown*, *Radar's Patch* and the forthcoming *Radar's Chequered History*.

Christine Rose is a former councillor of the Auckland Regional Council. She is a marine mammal advocate, an environmentalist, an artist and writer and a cheerleader for cycling.

Tom Scott is a columnist, cartoonist, author and playwright with numerous television programmes and films to his name including *Fallout*, *View from the Top*, *Footrot Flats: The Dog's Tale*, *Rage*, *Separation City* and the semi-autobiographical stage play *The Daylight Atheist*.

Scotty 'Sumo' Stevenson is a SKY Sport rugby commentator and editor of SKY *Sport – the Magazine*.

Sonja Yelich's first collection of poems, *Clung*, won the 2005 Jessie Mackay Award at the New Zealand Book Awards. She was Buddle Findlay Sargeson Fellow in 2010. She is the mother of four remarkable children.

Acknowledgements

This little history of a very big game owes a large debt to the work of Brian Sutton-Smith, who died earlier his year. His legacy is huge. Few scholars, if any, have done as much to understand the role of play in our lives.

Good people with wonderful stories made this project a constant pleasure. I'm grateful to them all for making the time to share their memories: Michèle A'Court, Jenine Abarbanel, Jacinda Ardern, Len Brown, Frank Bunce, Wallace Chapman, Peter FitzSimons, Rodney Hide, Robert Kelly, Josh Kronfeld, Michelle Langstone, Brendhan Lovegrove, Greg McGee, Bruce McLachlan, Robyn Malcolm, Midge Marsden, Scotty Morrison, Stacey Morrison, Roger Moses, Te Radar, Christine Rose, Tom Scott, James Sikora, Scotty Stevenson, Nat Torkington, Sam Ward and Sonja Yelich.

I thank the pupils of Devonport Primary School for their wonderful bullrush pictures, Sam Mayhew Photography for shots of the Tika Bullrush Pro-Am and especially Gordon McBride for his marvellous photos of the boys tearing into each other at Wellington College.

Listeners to Radio Live and Radio New Zealand contributed their memories too, and I thank them all for their entertaining contributions – none more so than that former inmate of Paparua prison.

I'm also grateful for recollections and world-weary wisdom from my two oldest friends, Nigel Hughes and Peter Whiteman; and grateful, for all their help, to Lesia Wallis and Ruth Spencer, who so perceptively see the shortcomings of the world and treat it so warmly all the same. My mother Penny also had bullrush memories. She gave me, in reading, the greatest of gifts. Dad – Tony – discouraged me, as this book relates, from a life in farming and I give thanks for that every day.

Getting this book onto paper was a happy, easy business thanks to highly capable and genuinely nice people: Madeleine James, Dexter Fry, Dana Brown, Eva Chan, Sandra Noakes and especially Finlay Macdonald, who is always calm, always wise, a great friend and the consummate publisher.

Most of all, Karren Beanland, who rightly says she doesn't get nearly enough credit for being willing to marry me, and our wonderful daughter, Mary-Margaret, who is dancing her way through life in a way that warms our hearts.